PENGUIN BOOKS
Negotiation Skills

Dennis Jenkins has had considerable experience in executive sales management, marketing and management roles for major organisations over many years, including the AMP Society and Marac. He has a BCom in Economics; a Teaching Diploma; is a Fellow of the Australian Insurance Institute and Associate Fellow of the NZIM. His professional memberships include the Institute of Directors, the American Society for Training and Development, and the American Management and Marketing Associations.

Dennis joined David Forman in 1986 and for several years tutored in sales, marketing and negotiation. As managing director, he continued to expand the company's range of programmes. After buying the company in 1990, Dennis and his wife, Frances, along with David Forman, developed and exported sales and negotiation programmes for the Australasian and North American markets.

As Executive Chairman, Dennis oversees all programme development and the tutorial team. He is a regular guest speaker at business functions and conferences.

NEGOTIATION SKILLS
Dennis Jenkins

Robert

Many thanks for your hospitality and conversation

Best regards

Dennis

02/06

For David, business coach and mentor; and
Frances, best friend, and business and life partner.

PENGUIN BOOKS
Penguin Books (NZ) Ltd, cnr Airborne and Rosedale Roads, Albany,
Auckland 1310, New Zealand
Penguin Books Ltd, 27 Wrights Lane, London W8 5TZ, England
Penguin USA, 375 Hudson Street, New York, NY 10014, United States
Penguin Books Australia Ltd, 487 Maroondah Highway, Ringwood, Australia
3134
Penguin Books Canada Ltd, 10 Alcorn Avenue, Toronto, Ontario, Canada M4V
3B2

Penguin Books Ltd, Registered Offices: Harmondsworth, Middlesex, England

First published by Penguin Books (NZ) Ltd, 1997

1 3 5 7 9 10 8 6 4 2

Copyright © Dennis Jenkins, 1997

The right of Dennis Jenkins to be identified as the author of this work in terms
of section 96 of the Copyright Act 1994 is hereby asserted.

Designed and typeset by Stewart Gardiner of Egan-Reid Ltd

Printed by Wright and Carman (NZ) Limited, Wellington

All rights reserved. Without limiting the rights under copyright reserved above,
no part of this publication may be reproduced, stored in or introduced
into a retrieval system, or transmitted, in any form or by any means
(electronic, mechanical, photocopying, recording or otherwise), without
the prior written permission of both the copyright owner and
the above publisher of this book.

Contents

Acknowledgements — 7
Introduction: the strategic view — 9
How to use this book — 15

1. Our negotiation mentality — 21
2. Creativity – building the best deals — 28
3. Structure and process — 37
4. You are in a negotiation – why? — 46
5. Outcomes — 54
6. The gaps – analysing the tension for change — 64
7. Variables – the ingredients of success — 71
8. What's it worth? — 80
9. What do we want to achieve? — 89
10. Your shopping list – bringing it all together — 97
11. Opening – initiate, gain, maintain — 105
12. Preconditioning – thinking way ahead — 112
13. Control the process – manage the outcome — 116
14. Expansion – the time for creativity — 128
15. Trading – unique to negotiation — 135
16. Finalising – putting the deal to bed — 147

17	When in difficulties	154
18	Power	161
19	Negotiating on price	168
20	Building trust and credibility	177
21	Communicating with power	182
22	What negotiations do you find yourself in?	189

In conclusion . . .	201
Appendix	204
About David Forman Training	221
Index/Glossary	223

Acknowledgements

The people behind this book

I first met David Forman in the early 1970s. He was busy establishing the training business on both sides of the Pacific, and developing and running sales, negotiation and management seminars for a number of international companies. I was one of his corporate clients, and he conducted seminars for us for over fifteen years. The company that I worked for was a leader in financial services, and it was my investment manager team that David first adapted his generic negotiation programme to. I was very fortunate to be exposed at this point in my own management career to a person who epitomised the very best in commercial experience, business acumen, academic excellence and psychology. His negotiation seminar was an integral part of most experienced salespeople's training and has remained a core programme in the organisation's seminar range throughout the world.

In the late 1980s the scope of the programme was widened to ensure it met the needs of all corporate disciplines, and today it is used by a wide range of companies from most industry sectors. It covers purchasing, selling, production, finance, personnel and marketing. It has been customised for many companies requiring a specific industry slant or type of negotiation emphasised.

To meet the demands of the business world, the programme has been continually updated and expanded. This has only been possible through the continued support of the programme from our clients, and their staff, who have attended the seminars and given us valuable feedback. This feedback always comes initially to our local programme managers, and it is to them that the credit must go for the high level of acceptance and recognition of the negotiation programme as the industry leader. In particular, the current Pacific team – Lyn Adam, Mark Brewer, Dennis Cowell, Jan de Zoete, Bruce Dickey, Gavin Houston, Roger McGill, Martyn McKessar, Beth Nyman and Colin Sander; and the Canadian team – Murray Janewski, C. S. (Chuck) Steeves, Tom Watson and Paul Yuck, who consult with our corporate clients and facilitate the programmes.

To all my international colleagues who ensure that our negotiation participants and graduates are looked after; to Rochelle Young for managing the editorial process; to Frances Jenkins and Ruth Middleton for their continuous support and encouragement; and to Bernice Beachman and her team at Penguin Books – my grateful thanks.

The theme of this book is based on the highly successful David Forman Negotiation Breakthroughs programme. The text of the book is however written with the intention of making the subject and practice of negotiation more accessible and enjoyable. We do after all spend a large part of our lives managing transactions with others, and we owe it to them and ourselves to do it well.

Dennis Jenkins
October 1997

Introduction: the strategic view

Negotiation skills . . . do you need them?

I'm a TV drama fan, and I enjoy a couple of hospital dramas – like 'Chicago Hope'. A recent episode had one of the world's foremost heart surgeons battling it out with her seven-year-old daughter. The subject was a change of school. In mother's eyes, the proposed change was the best and only option – enrolment at the most prestigious private girls' school in the state. She used all her contacts, her position, her very powerful persuasive manner and plain dogged persistence to get the interview and entry examination arranged. Her daughter was a very reluctant participant in all of this – in fact she was very happy, thank you, with the nice school she was at and did not wish to go to any other school, no matter how up-market it was!

Now, it may have been possible to persuade the young lady at this point by applying well-known negotiation techniques (nothing underhand, just good old-fashioned common-sense discussion based on two-way communication and consideration of feelings as well as facts). But no, the total weight of the mother's considerable power came down on the negotiation – implied threats, wheedling, false promises, charm, 'I'm only doing the best for you,' and so on. So what was the response of the daughter? Totally predictable! Defiant, sulky, 'you don't love me,' every rejection – both real and imagined – thrown back at her mother. And even worse, a very deliberate and calculated failure of the entrance examination! So mother was back to the beginning, but this time behind the eight-ball with the school as well!

Now, this situation could have turned nasty, as family disagreements often do when not managed properly, but the daughter came to the rescue after the mother adopted a more nurturing-parent style. Allowing the youngster to express her feelings freely, without being interrupted for a change, the situation suddenly became a classic negotiation. 'If I pass the exam, and agree to go to this school, will you buy me the new school bag in the pink colour I like?' Bingo! Sleepless nights, tears, sulks, utter frustration – for both mother and daughter – resolved in a simple exchange.

Why was I intrigued with this example of a negotiation? Simply because it had all the elements of the process in one situation. And all showing how not to do it, right up to the end: planning non-existent, poor preconditioning, one-way communication, bullying, threats, no willingness to listen to the other side's point of view, no creative problem-solving, no exploration of other issues, a disregard of feelings – in short a complete lack of understanding of what negotiation is about, and thus a haphazard process. In this case they eventually arrived at a mutually happy outcome, but that was mere chance, not planned.

Now I want you to think back over the past week. What discussions have you had with your partner, family, social or business colleague, customer or supplier that have revolved around getting an agreement between you both on some matter? It may have been as simple as: 'If you get dinner tonight, I'll sweep the path tomorrow,' or as complex as a business deal involving the purchase and installation of a new printing machine, or just a very regular meeting working out the allocation of resources, in people, time, and money terms, with a colleague. How many have you had? I'd venture to guess that you can think of several simple personal situations, and at least one in a non-personal environment.

My next question is obvious. Do you think that you managed this transaction in the very best possible way? Was the final outcome exactly as you had planned? Did you even have a planned outcome to check that you had indeed achieved what you had wanted? Was the other party – partner, child, colleague, supplier or customer – happy with the final deal? How do you know? Could you have asked for something else that would have made your outcome even better? Was there something that you could have offered the other party that would have enhanced the deal for them, made them feel more committed to you, yet have cost you nothing?

So my next statement is also obvious. Virtually every day of our lives, in personal, social and business situations, we are in a classic negotiation situation – whether we realise it or not! So it is well worth us making sure that we are getting the very best from these transactions. This is not a selfish statement. Far from it. A good negotiator not only looks after their own interests, but manages the transaction so that both parties get as much as possible out of the arrangement. A simple example will show this in action.

A neighbour was doing some renovations and asked if they could store some furniture in our shed for a few weeks. They'd pay a nominal rental. A simple transaction, like most, could have been agreed to then and there, with both sides happy with the outcome. But thinking ahead, I knew that he would be using a plasterer. Our house had a filled-in wall that with a little bit of extra work by me could be ready for plastering, a job I always leave to the professionals. And the cost of getting in a plasterer for a small one-off job would be relatively expensive. So we did a classic but very simple negotiation. He got the plasterer to quote for both jobs, and we calculated the extra for doing mine was $100. This was about one-third of the cost for a one-off job, which of course would have had to include travelling time, etc. He was willing to pay me about $300 for the storage. So we did a simple exchange – he paid for my plastering and I gave him the storage free.

I'm sure you will recognise this type of simple negotiation transaction that you do regularly with family, friends and colleagues. But always look for the next opportunity. In this particular instance, a semi-retired friend had been unable to do his normal outdoor work through illness, but could work indoors. It turned out that he was pretty good with hammers and paint brushes as well as his gardening tools, and I ended up with him supervising the total job, including the painting which I detest. So a win for several parties – the neighbour, the plasterer, the friend and me. Not to mention my wife who is usually frustrated by my procrastination on such jobs!

In summary then, it is essential that we are good negotiators. We use the skills and process every day. We must ensure that our dealings with family, friends and business partners achieve the very best outcome for them and us, for why waste opportunities to build better relationships? Which naturally leads us to consider the next question – what is negotiation?

Negotiation defined . . . is it any more than just getting a good deal?

We've been looking at negotiation as a transaction. And it is. But it is a specific kind of transaction. Let's, therefore, be quite clear about the unique features of negotiation.

If you ask your son to mow the lawn, and he accepts the request with a simple 'yes', that is not a negotiation, but a request or order met. If, however, he had responded to your request with: 'I'd be happy to mow the lawn if you would help me with my maths homework tonight,' you would find yourself in a classic negotiation situation. Of course, as his parent, you can easily reject the chance of negotiation and just repeat the request, which many of us do out of habit, but why not consider the wider opportunities it offers? How about taking up his proposal but making it really work for both of you. 'OK, I'll work with you on your homework if you do the lawn before lunch and tidy up your desk before dinner.' Now that's more like it! So what is the essential difference? The second and third transactions have an element of exchange, or give and take. And this is the essential difference between many transactions and negotiation – the ability to exchange, or in negotiation terms 'to trade or bargain'.

We engage most days in buy-sell transactions. Are they negotiations? Let's have a look at a simple buy-sell situation. You go into the hardware store to buy a new saw blade. You choose one from the shelf, take it to the checkout counter, the salesperson rings it up, swipes your credit card, wraps it up and bids you have a happy day. You bought; they sold. Not a negotiation, as nothing was traded – all you did was pay the asking price.

An element of trading, and thus negotiation, would have been introduced if you had said: 'I usually pay by credit card, but what amount of discount would you give me if I paid cash this time?' Now you have introduced the opportunity for a simple negotiation to occur. A simple response might be: 'Sorry, we don't give discounts,' in which case it's up to you to accept that as fact or try something else as an exchange. Or they may not wish to give discounts, which after all come straight off their bottom line, but may offer an alternative like: 'I'm sorry but we don't give discounts, but we do have a saw-sharpening service and I can give you a voucher to have your blade sharpened at no cost.' They may even add that this normally costs $20, and you will be very happy to accept this as it represents a 20% discount on the blade. (We'll cover the relative cost to the store in Chapter 8. This, in fact, is a good arrangement for them too.)

This transaction is now a simple negotiation, which may be completed by you accepting, or expanded further by you proposing some other action. For example, you may say: 'Thank you for that offer, but last year I bought a saw-sharpening jig from you, and I look after my own blades. However, my skill-saw needs a service, and that usually costs about $20 – would your voucher cover that?' A classic simple negotiation is evolving.

So we can see that transactions without the element of exchange or trade are not negotiations – though they can be turned into negotiations by either party introducing an aspect or item that can be traded. We call these variables. We'll be looking at variables in great detail in Chapter 7, but for the moment just think of them as items that can be changed, sometimes only a little (like the time for the lawn to be mowed and the homework done) or a lot (like when the skill-saw could be serviced).

If your boss gives you a raise, is that a negotiation? Obviously not, if it is a simple case of you saying 'Thank you' or even 'Thanks, I'm pleased you finally recognise my worth.' But you may be in a position to turn it into a negotiation by saying: 'Thanks for the offer, but I was wanting to discuss the option of an extra month's leave this year to visit family overseas. Perhaps we could look at the question of leave in conjunction with the pay rise you've proposed.' Note how extra variables have been introduced, quite simply and reasonably. This has now become a simple negotiation situation, with variables that could include a rise, holiday with pay, holiday without pay, extra leave, payment for the trip in lieu of monetary rise, fringe benefit tax, time of leave, replacement staff, workloads, training, overseas business visit, etc.

In summary, let's look at some of the definitions of negotiation which truly represent the essence of negotiation.

Getting what we want by enabling others to get what they want. The word 'enabling' indicates the willingness and ability to change aspects or items involved.

A process of bargaining to reach an outcome. The word 'bargaining' means exchange, barter, trade, give and take.

Trading variable for variable with the aim of arriving at the most advantageous outcome for each party. This specifically covers the trading of variables.

Provided we think of negotiation in terms of an exchange of things of value in order to reach an outcome that both parties can accept, we will be able to manage the process of negotiation. The aim of this book is to provide you with the necessary concepts, structures and processes of negotiation to enable you to become more skilled and confident in any negotiation situation you find yourself in.

There is one more distinction that we need to make. Problem-solving is not negotiation. Problems may arise within a negotiation, and the problem-solving process may be used to resolve it, but you can solve a problem without resorting to any aspect of negotiation. Problem-solving is where both parties have a common objective (such as two neighbours discussing the options of removing an old fence on their boundary); negotiation is where both parties have a different objective (such as one wanting the old fence removed, while the other wants it repaired). Neither are right or wrong, they are just different situations – common objective or different objective. We will describe a simple problem-solving process that you can use within a negotiation in Chapter 2.

How to use this book

It's structured for easy reference . . .
You want to be able to find something quickly and easily. A negotiation may be coming up next week that you want to be sure you are preparing for correctly. You can search the Index/Glossary at the back of the book first. This will refer you to the relevant chapter. Or you may have had a less than satisfactory meeting with a business partner, and felt you could have handled the negotiation better, particularly at the beginning. Again, a search of the Index/Glossary will give you the chapter about beginnings, and references to difficulties you may have experienced. Although negotiation is a process, and therefore has a logical sequence to it, most aspects are covered more than once using different examples to make it as relevant to your particular situation as possible. So use the Index/Glossary – it's there to help!

As a quick guide to what's covered in each chapter, there is a summary of the aspects at the beginning of each chapter. Each topic is then under a sub-heading. But remember that your interest area may well be covered elsewhere, so always use the Index/Glossary for a full coverage. Good negotiators want to know everything! We all feel pretty bad about negotiations that didn't turn out well, and doubly so if the fault was a lack of forethought on our part!

The Index/Glossary lists the main terms used in negotiations. This is a delightful read by itself. In fact I think many negotiators like to use the terminology to give them power – just like a technician likes to use technical terms and jargon for both power and comfort! But like most other human activities, negotiation is really just plain old common sense, put into a language that explains where you are at, and what you are doing. So don't be put off by the jargon – learn to use it when you're preparing for any situation, whether it be a major business deal or a discussion with the neighbour about the boundary fence. After all, if negotiation is about getting agreement between parties, then at least use a common language! You may even find that you get a better outcome. Teenagers, and even young children, respond in a very positive way when the arrangement you are working out with them is couched in real-life negotiation language. They manage their emotions more positively when they understand the process that you are working through with them. And they are often far more creative than we give them credit for! So become familiar with the language of negotiation! It's a major confidence booster, especially when you get a difficult one.

As a quick read, or for an overview . . . skip the rest of this chapter.

Although this book isn't a novel, it is able to be read straight through to get an overall feel of the essence of negotiation. Some readers will already be skilled negotiators, and this book is just part of your continuous personal updating process. So a quick read will suit you, and you can mark anything of specific interest to you for later study. Others like to get the big picture of a subject first, before getting down to the details. So a quick read is perfectly appropriate. Quick readers should go straight to Chapter 1. Come back to this page when you want to do some serious study and skills development.

If you're serious about improving your negotiation skills . . . read on!

This book is designed as a learning guide. A detailed study, coupled with real-world negotiation practice, will significantly improve the beginner's understanding and outcomes. Advanced students of negotiation can enhance their skills and outcomes by incremental improvements.

At the beginning of each chapter is a box setting out the essence of the topic covered in the chapter. Read the statements thoughtfully, and endeavour to get the bigger picture of the topic in your mind. Think about what each sentence says, and relate it to your own negotiation experience.

Then move into the body of the chapter. Although this is designed to be read in a continuous way, there are periodic questions in the form of 'What do you think . . .?' When you reach one of these, don't skip it! Think about what is behind the question, and formulate an answer in your mind. Although there are no formal answers to these questions, they will ensure you get your mind around the essential idea or process. It means you are taking an active part in your own learning and self-evaluation.

At the end of each chapter

The Key Points Summary emphasises the main concepts, processes, skills, etc. For you, this should be thoroughly studied, for if you can absorb these messages you will find your real-world negotiations are far more controlled and satisfying. The transfer of the skills from the mind to the actual negotiation event will become more rapid and more effective. As your confidence grows, so will your power.

Following the Key Point Summary, there is a self-test. Depending on the topic, they take the form of multiple-choice questions, agree/disagree statements, or an activity based on the topic. Answers or suggested responses are included in the Appendix.

80/20 . . . Pareto again!

You all know the Pareto principle – 80% of the work is done by 20% of the people; 80% of the profit is produced by 20% of the products; 80% of our customers produce 20% of our sales, etc! Well, there's no difference in this ratio as it relates to success. Numerous studies reported over the years from a variety of sources indicate that successful people have a higher level of *will do* factors than *can do* factors. Whether it's exactly 80/20 is irrelevant – the point is that attitude counts for significantly more than aptitude. Ask any sports team coach!

A warning though – you can have all the attitude and will do factors in the world, but without the aptitudes, skills and knowledge, the can do factors, you will not get very far. They rely on each other for total achievement.

To help you keep a track on how you are going on both these factors, we use a success model, Figure 1. I suggest you refer to it each time you complete the You Try It exercises.

The three rectangles around the outside are the three can do or aptitude factors. You get knowledge through study (such as this book), attending seminars, coaching sessions, talking with knowledgeable people, watching educational videos, etc. You gain skills through practice, and the more you practise using the correct understanding and skill set, the better you become in the actual doing. From these two you develop judgement, or wisdom. You can improve your judgement quite quickly if you review your negotiation experiences immediately they finish, and make notes on what you did well and areas needing improvement. It is very helpful if you have someone to advise you here – perhaps a partner, or a friend or boss. Their judgement may be better and more objective than yours! By the way, if you are in paid employment, judgement is what you are primarily paid for!

The inner circle are the will do or attitudinal factors – accounting for that 80% of success. Your attitude to negotiation and the people you are dealing with needs to be positive; your personal, and business, value systems need to be understood and internalised, and you need to be confident about your knowledge, skills and judgement as a negotiator. Your personal drive factors should be strong, with a determination to succeed, and generally a 'do it' mentality. Perhaps needed more in negotiation than other human interactions is a high level of control over your emotions. This means that you are able to block your habitual reactions to events and people, and respond in a mature, appropriate way that keeps you in control of yourself and the situation. That lovely line from Rudyard Kipling's 'If' sums it up – 'If you can keep your head when all about you are losing theirs and blaming it on you . . .'

We use the success model on a number of our management seminars, and most graduates continue to use it in their personal and professional lives. It's a never filled model – the moment you think you've got it all is the moment you've stopped

Figure 1: Success model

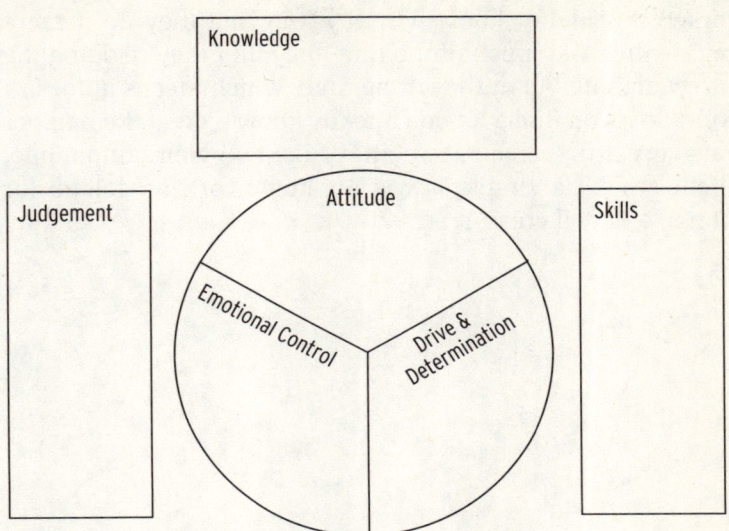

learning! So we suggest you complete this model for yourself at the end of each chapter. You can then keep a track on how you are going in each area, and you will quickly note how they interact. What usually happens is that an increased understanding (knowledge) leads to confidence in trying it out (skill practice) which reaffirms a positive approach (attitude) and increases the desire to repeat the success (drive). As judgement improves after each negotiation review, control over the feelings of self and others increases (emotional control). They are very interdependent!

If you're a continuous improvement fan . . . check your levels at the end of each chapter, and at the conclusion of every major negotiation.

There is one other service David Forman Training offers the serious student. If you have a particular question about any aspect of negotiation, you may fax our Help Line. Details are on page 222.

When business people attend our negotiation seminars, they find they already have a base of knowledge about negotiation. Some will know more than others. But they often find that what they knew was only half the facts, and it was making them less effective. Or they were doing some activity that worked, but didn't know why; by knowing they do it more confidently. And much of the time they find they're doing the correct activity but at the wrong time, which means it doesn't work! So if you find a lot you already know – great. Remember that every extra percentage point you put on your bottom line, whether it be a simple lawns for homework or dollars for volume – is real cream!

1 | Our negotiation mentality

▶Our attitude to negotiation is largely determined by our past experiences. We develop approaches that range between highly competitive and over collaborative. Our attitude and approach become predictable behaviours. Becoming a skilled negotiator requires us to block our habitual reactions, and be flexible within each negotiation situation. We can manage conflict through adopting assertive styles and behaviours. Adopting an abundance mentality will enhance negotiation outcomes.

Competitive or collaborative . . . a hard-nose or a wimp?

Whether we are naturally competitive or naturally collaborative, we all remember dealing with others who are at the extremes. And they are both uncomfortable. On the one hand, the competitive person seems more intent on winning than on the outcome, whereas the collaborative person seems to be doomed to giving everything away. You want to get away from the competitive person as quickly as possible in case they also take the shirt off your back, and you want to return some of what you got from the collaborator because you feel sorry for them!

Obviously, neither extreme is appropriate. Even international negotiations are now conducted in a non-confrontational environment – decades of experience have shown that somewhere in between, or at least moving between, the extremes of competitive and collaborative there is usually a reasonable and acceptable outcome.

That's not to say that competitive tactics are not appropriate. If one party is being deliberately provocative, then a threat of dire consequences by the other may be necessary to put the negotiations back on track. Look at the news on TV or in the newspaper for current examples.

There are negotiation situations where the past strongly influences the present. Many union/employer negotiations are still competitive, with heavy use of negative preconditioning, outrageous demands from each party, delay tactics, threats of strikes and redundancies, hidden agendas, excessive use of power, and generally a high level of mutual suspicion. This book does not deal with that extreme type of negotiation style, though in Chapters 17 and 18 you will find some methods to manage those competitive situations and people.

We shouldn't tolerate those who are overly collaborative either. You can't effectively negotiate with someone who just gives in. You may think it's wonderful, but think of the consequences. If they won't discuss aspects fully or explore different options, or aren't willing to voice their concerns, what chance do you have of getting the best deal – for both of you? You'll come out with a mediocre deal that you're not really happy with, but wondering why not. I've seen good negotiators literally pick up a wimp, sit them in front of a flip chart, and start doing their side of the negotiation for them – just to get them out of their collaborative mindset and habitual behaviour. So this book does not deal with the extreme collaborative style either – you can do that without our help if you wish!

In practice, you'll find the best negotiators work somewhere in between those two extremes – what is called the competitive-collaborative continuum. Some call it consultative negotiation, but don't get stuck with being in the middle! Be flexible. You may have to become quite hard-nosed with a supplier on one contract, but can be quite helpful on another the following week.

When you're living or working closely with the people you negotiate with, you are likely to favour the collaborative end. Think carefully of the effect your stance could have on the relationship. For example, would you be blatantly unreasonable with a close neighbour? Of course not! What about the building inspector in your area if you're the local plumber? Or if you are the line boss of an extremely valuable employee who reports functionally to the powerful technical manager?

However, if it's a one-off deal and you're unlikely to meet the other party again, you can adopt a more competitive approach. A typical example would be buying or selling a house. Competitive doesn't necessarily mean nasty, but buyer or seller can try for every advantage they can get. Buying or selling anything where no ongoing relationship is required can be more competitive, without necessarily suffering any adverse consequences.

> We first make our habits, and then our habits make us. **John Dryden**

Predictability... the 95% factor

One of the problems we suffer when we negotiate is our predictability. We formed patterns of behaviour when we were babies, like whining or charm, to get our own way, and some of us still preserve them. I'm sure you know of the friend who always seems to be in disagreement with someone – one week it's their neighbour they're moaning about, next week they're complaining about their boss, a month later they tell you they had an argument with the power company. They're predictable, and you have been told by others: 'They've always been like that – ever since school.' Psychologists tell us that 95% of our behaviour is habitual. So what is predictable about you? And is it helpful to you, or a hindrance? Do people get defensive when they are dealing with you because you come on overly strong? Or do you get put upon by others who see you constantly as a soft touch? So review your habitual negotiation behaviours. You can learn to block your habitual reactions if you are aware of them. A good way to start is to simply ask two or three close friends or colleagues how they view you as a negotiator.

Abundance or scarcity... what's your view of the world?

You have probably seen the picture of a glass half-filled with water, with the caption 'Is it half-full or half-empty?' And the explanation that goes with it – if you see it as half-full you are an abundance thinker, if you see it as half-empty you are a scarcity thinker. The point is that abundance thinkers consider that there is enough to go around, that sharing resources is possible, that it is feasible to achieve more than the parts by adding them together (synergy). Scarcity thinkers consider that there are limited resources, that if one gains it will be at the expense of another, so they are reluctant to share. They operate from the zero-sum mentality (the net gains for each side will always add up to zero).

Good negotiators generally adopt an abundance mentality. The reason for this is simple. Even when there are scarce resources, they know from experience that there are always options and alternatives which can convert the limited resources into satisfactory parts to be shared between the parties. Having faith in their ability to creatively expand the variables available provides the impetus to search for more and better ways of achieving a worthwhile outcome.

Typically, competitive negotiators are scarcity thinkers, whilst collaborative thinkers are abundance thinkers. Which are you?

Conflict . . . does it bother you?

In most of your social or professional negotiations you will meet conflict. The fact that you are in a negotiation rather than a discussion or problem-solving situation means you have differing outcome objectives, so conflict is almost built in. But it's how you manage that conflict that is critical.

Good negotiators should be assertive – with their words, their tone and their body language. Figure 2 illustrates the four approaches you can adopt. Which approach do you typically adopt? Do you change depending on who you are negotiating with?

Let's consider how these different approaches sound in a typical negotiation.

Supplier: 'I know you ordered last week, and paid for it, but our truck was late back from an urgent job which means your delivery will be done on Monday. I'm sorry I can't help.'
Customer – Aggressive: 'Utterly unacceptable! Get it there today or you can give me my money back right now.'
Customer – Passive: 'That's a shame. I really needed it this weekend. Oh well, I guess I'll have to wait.'

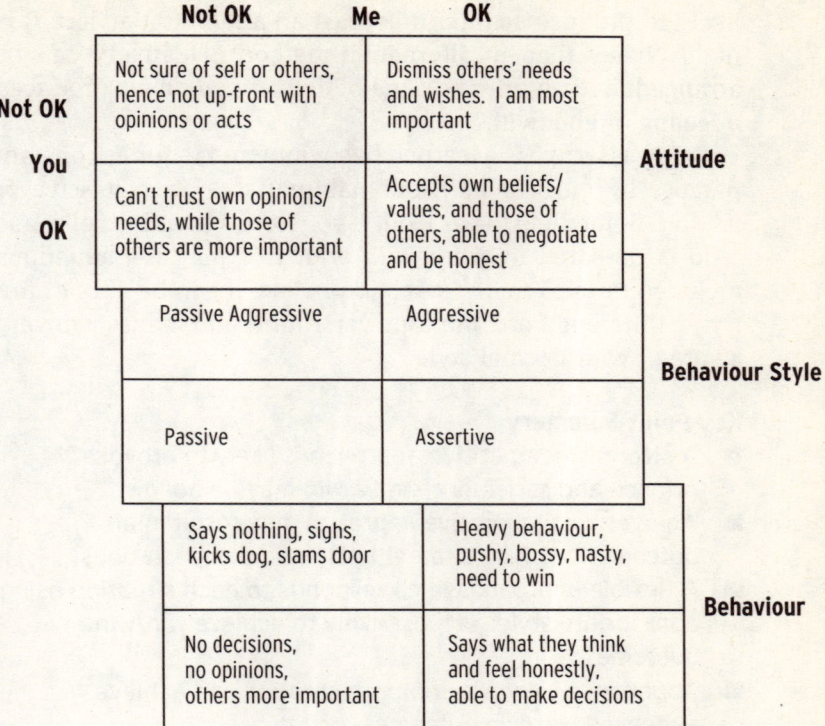

Figure 2: Assertion matrix

Customer – Passive Aggressive: 'Huh!' and stamps the floor.
Customer – Assertive: 'The delivery was promised for today, and it is needed today for a weekend event. What alternative delivery method can you arrange today? I'd be prepared to accept an evening delivery, but not later than eight o'clock.'

What response could you expect from these words and tone messages? The first is likely to get either an aggressive response which will escalate the hostility, or a defensive one, but still may not produce the delivery needed. The second will just meet with another 'Yes, I'm sorry, it is a shame' with no action. The third achieves nothing, and probably doesn't even relieve the tension.

The fourth, assertive in both words and tone, is the most

likely to produce action, or at least an attempt at action. It is highly likely that an alternative method of delivery can be arranged, and an offer on time of delivery will have produced a feeling of goodwill.

Being assertive is a learned behaviour and requires constant practise by most of us if our habitual style is aggressive or passive. Something to work on! If you have a friend or colleague who is prepared to work with you, role play the situations included in the You Try It section below. It can be a lot of fun trying different word and tone variations, and makes you very aware of your normal style.

Key Point Summary
- A strongly competitive approach is likely to provoke offence and resistance, and a win may be hollow
- An overly collaborative approach may result in an outcome that fails to meet bottom-line expectations
- A flexible approach which responds to each situation using appropriate styles is most likely to achieve win/win outcomes
- Abundance thinkers are more creative and achieve enhanced win/win outcomes
- Assertive verbal and non-verbal behaviours are best in all negotiations

▶ YOU TRY IT

Here are some common negotiating behaviours – verbal and non-verbal. Indicate the approach of each. (Answers in the Appendix.)

❶ Child with clenched hands on hips and stamping their right foot: 'If you don't watch out, I won't swap anything with you!'

❷ Boss to staff member, seated in interview room at a round table: 'We both have different objectives on this one, but we need to resolve it. What do you think?'

❸ Parent, sitting in their chair, hands behind head, legs crossed – to teenager: 'You'd better do something about it right now, because if you don't there's no way I'll even consider an increase in your allowance.'

4 Colleague with head down: 'I wonder if you could possibly consider letting me have that machine a week earlier, but don't worry if it's too much bother.'

5 'I think I can see a way out of this. Why don't we both reschedule the delivery dates? Would you be able to arrange that at your end, if I could do that here?'

6 Customer to supplier, pointing index finger at wall chart: 'Any fool can see that we required it yesterday – are your people thick? You'd better make it damn quick, or you won't get another order out of me.'

7 Customer to supplier, standing with open arms: 'Well Robert, you've got us all into a fine pickle! As we agreed last week, we required it yesterday. I feel we've been let down. What do you propose to do to rectify it?'

8 Neighbour to neighbour, over fence: 'Michelle, I know that you can't do anything about it, but would you mind very much fixing that hole in your fence as your dog keeps getting through and makes a mess on my lawn. Not that it really matters much of course, it's just that I have to clear it up before Anna gets home.'

9 Town planner to architect, reviewing plans for a house alteration: 'Mark, you've given me a headache here! There's no way I can pass that stairs design. However, I've pulled out a couple of alternative designs that you and your client may be happy to consider – both of which meet the guidelines. Will that help you?'

10 'My company couldn't even look at it – it's a preposterous request! I'm surprised that you of all people would even consider asking! It makes a mockery of the whole arrangement.'

2 | Creativity – building the best deals

▶An abundance thinker is more creative. A creative approach in a negotiation almost invariably results in an expanded outcome. Creativity is contagious! Anyone can develop their creative ability. Brainstorming and mind-mapping are two simple and effective activities which are easily adapted to negotiation situations. Negotiation and problem-solving are different, and each requires different processes.

A creative approach . . . your most precious asset

'I wish I'd been encouraged to think like that about negotiations' is a typical comment from graduates as they leave the seminar after three days of intense learning and practice. 'I could have got a much better deal for us, and the other party would have been delighted with my creative way of handling the situation.'

Negotiation is a creative activity. Have you ever listened to people planning their holiday? They've researched every way to get there; every conceivable side visit or attraction brochure has been read and discussed; they've got their wardrobe planned for each day; they've bought new suitcases – and it's still weeks before they leave. And they're only going away for 10 days! Yet we go into important negotiations with just the bare facts, with a minimum of preparation and, I'm sorry to

> Most good ideas sparkle in simplicity, so much so that everyone wonders why no one ever did that before. **Estée Lauder**

say, with little if any creativity. Why not? Isn't the outcome important? We all agree it is, but creativity and negotiation don't seem to go together. Wrong! If you study the really successful business negotiations, the ones that worked for both sides and stood the test of time, you will find a significant amount of innovation and lateral thinking was involved before the final deal was agreed.

Next time you are in a family negotiation, introduce some creativity and see what happens. A business acquaintance of mine had a 17-year-old whose life at that time revolved around clothes, boys, parties and the telephone. The mother decided she'd paid out enough for designer labels, that her own best clothes were being borrowed without an ask, and the telephone was tied up till 10 o'clock virtually every night. So she decided to negotiate some changes – but as creatively as possible. She certainly didn't want her daughter walking out!

The outcome contained some surprises. The daughter committed herself to an extra hour of study per night, which replaced one hour on the phone; preparing the evening meal on Sunday; driving the younger brother to band practice on Wednesday night, and bringing him home; ironing all the shirts and blouses once a week; and four days during the next school holidays helping her father archive his business records. In turn, the mother, father and brother committed themselves to not nagging about the state of her room; the mother agreed to lend her some outfits on the condition that they were washed or dry-cleaned before being returned; she would have the phone to herself for one hour each night; her private petrol would be subsidised in the form of a mileage allowance; and she would get paid for her holiday work. I understand that this arrangement worked out well while she was still at college, and has undergone only minor changes in her first year of university.

> Imagination is more important than knowledge. **Albert Einstein**

Why is creativity required? Because variables need to be massaged – split up, separated into parts, repackaged, expanded, linked with other variables, recosted and so on. It is only by being creative with the parts of a negotiation that you can enhance the whole. And your proactive creativity will encourage the other party to be innovative too.

Whole-brain thinking ... getting those cells working

There are many books about creativity for readers who want to explore the topic in depth. In essence, the brain has incredible powers. We can tap it to become more creative, to learn more effectively and to improve our memory. Many psychologists believe that we proactively use less than 10% of our brain power – that leaves us with tremendous potential! How about we just increase it to 20%?

Our brain has two halves, called the right and left hemispheres. The right hemisphere is the holistic mode and deals in thinking. It perceives and expresses visual, spatial and musical patterns, feelings and emotions. The left hemisphere is the logical mode. It controls analytical thought and verbal responses. It deals with information in a linear, logical, step-by-step process.

Fortunately for us, the two hemispheres talk to each other.

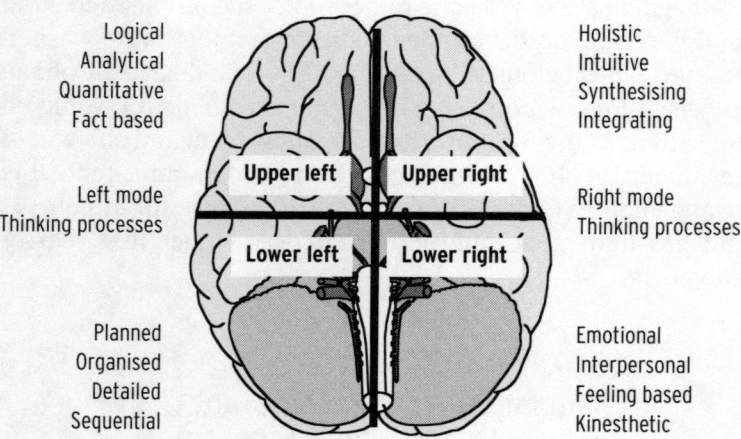

Figure 3: The human brain Courtesy Priority Management

> I not only use all the brains that I have, but all that I can borrow. **Woodrow Wilson**

They work in a complementary way and we are thus able to use what is called 'whole-brain' thinking. Ned Herrmann, the father of brain dominance technology, explains that the brain has in fact four structures rather than just two. These four paired structures consist of the two cerebral hemispheres and the two halves of the limbic system. Thankfully they're all connected! (If you're interested in whole-brain technology, read Ned Herrmann's *The Creative Brain*. It's a fascinating read!)

You have probably developed a left or right brain dominance, or preference, which means you are more 'comfortable' with one sort of thinking than the other. For example, research has shown that lawyers, engineers, bankers and bureaucrats tend to be predominantly left-brained, whereas writers, artists, musicians and entrepreneurs tend to be predominantly right-brained.

Brainstorming is the term used when we have an intensive discussion to solve problems or generate ideas. Although you can do it by yourself, a small group will generally achieve more as each person stimulates the others. It is useful to record the ideas where everyone can see them, so have a large sheet of paper, or flip chart or white-board with you.

Now, there are certain rules for brainstorming – mainly to stop those of us of whatever brain preference from dominating the generation of ideas!

Rules for brainstorming

1. No criticism
There is no evaluation or criticism during the idea-generating phase. The goal is to have a plethora of possibilities on the table for consideration.

2. Freewheeling is encouraged and welcomed
Participants are encouraged to blurt out whatever wild, strange or seemingly mundane idea that comes to mind. What at first

sounds crazy or impractical, may contain the germ of a great solution.

3. Go for quantity
The more ideas the better. Rule of thumb: if the group generates five or six ideas a minute, you'll probably end up with useful solutions.

4. Combine and improve
Encourage participants to build on one another's ideas – called 'piggybacking' – and to look for ways to combine two or more ideas that have already been offered and recorded.

Mind-mapping . . . an essential tool of trade
Our memory is arranged in millions of interconnecting networks. So any event, word or image can be retrieved from any point by a large number of different routes. One way of bringing together information and ideas stored in each hemisphere is by mind-mapping.

The mind-map is a creative tool for organising thinking, taking notes and improving memory. In negotiation, it is particularly useful during the preparation stage when you are searching for all the variables, sorting them into common areas, and splitting each one into as many parts as possible to improve your ability to trade them. It is also a valuable tool when a group of people wish to share ideas about a topic. The mind-map format allows everyone to contribute at the same time – particularly useful if you are involved in a team negotiation. Even family, social and neighbour negotiations benefit from using mind-maps when discussing the variables. Kids love them – it makes negotiation a creative activity for them, and you'd be surprised what they come up with which relieves you of some hard bargaining! In a business setting, mind-mapping is non-confrontational, and we've seen potentially difficult negotiations become quite collaborative when the neutral mind-map format was put on a flip chart.

Figure 4 shows how mind-maps can be used. For a detailed coverage of mind-mapping, read Tony Buzan's *The Mind Map Book* (BBC, 1995). He is the founder of mind-mapping

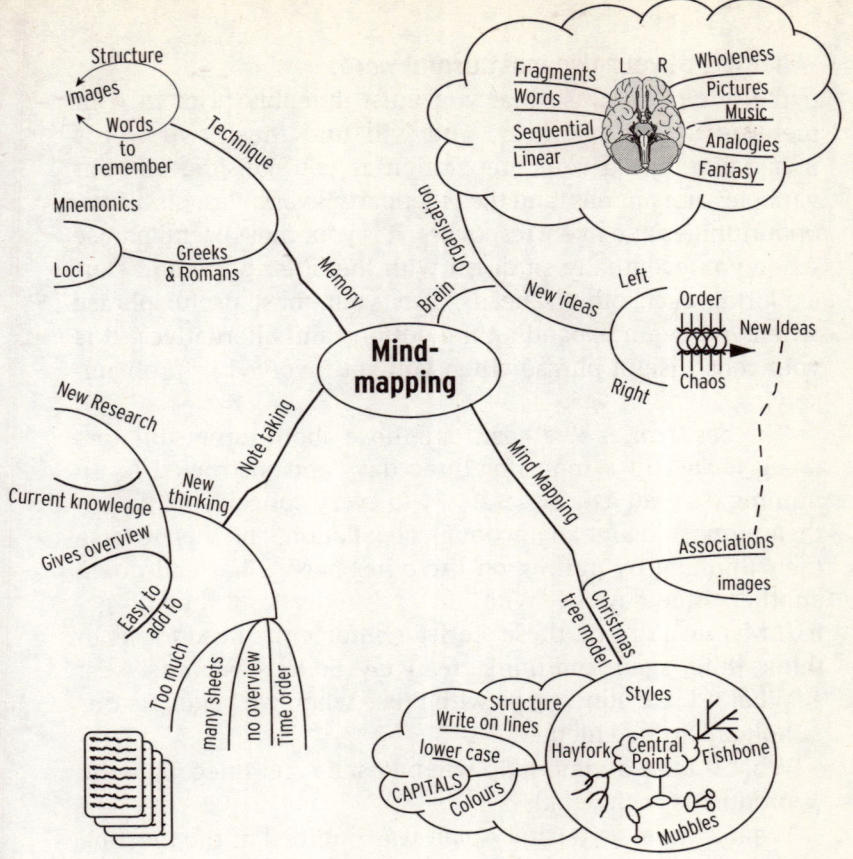

Figure 4: Mind-mapping Courtesy Priority Management

and the author of several best-selling books about the mind, memory and brainpower. Another interesting variation is Ingemar Svantesson's *Mind Mapping and Memory* (Swan Communications, 1989).

Because mind-mapping links both hemispheres, it also improves our memory. We're using the left's functions of observation, concentration, classification and memory with the right's functions of visualisation, association-linking and substitution. Even drawing a mind-map will help memorising. Many students are now taught mind-mapping to make their note-taking faster and easier, with more effective visual and memory recall.

'What if' ... your two most useful words

If there is one phrase that you must indelibly print in your memory it's 'What if . . .' You will find these two words invaluable during your preparation as you consider all your variables and options, and the other party's variables, problems, opportunities and likely responses. It is your most useful phrase when you eventually sit down with the other party and start exploring each other's needs. It is your most useful phrase when you begin expanding the options and alternatives. It is your most useful phrase when you get involved in problem-solving.

The best stories I've heard are those about top negotiators being locked in a room for three days and instructed to do nothing else but ask 'What if . . .' to every conceivable part of their proposition for an upcoming negotiation, and then reverse their thinking by putting on the other party's hat and doing another three days of 'What if . . .' I understand they do get fed! Mythical or not, these stories reinforce the need for us to think, think again and think creatively. So let's ask ourselves:

- 'What if I use mind-maps with Steve when we negotiate our holiday arrangements?'
- 'What if I use a mind-map when Rosalie and I negotiate the product launch details?'
- 'What if the new territory plan was outlined at the meeting using a mind-map?'
- 'What if Ruth and Murray mind-mapped a capital expenditure plan with the computer team before they negotiated the new loan?'
- 'What if I could provide the exact costings to Henry before we start the negotiations?'

Convinced? The use of these two words is endless!

Problem-solving ... a simple way-out process

We covered the point in the Introduction that problem-solving was not negotiation, but that within a negotiation a problem may arise that needs to be solved. Remember the distinction was that a negotiation involves two or more parties with different objectives – that is why they are negotiating.

In a problem-solving situation, the parties have the same

objective. So within a negotiation, a problem over one variable may arise that needs resolving and both parties have the same objective on that particular issue. Let's take getting delicate machinery into an office tower under construction for example. Both supplier and customer have the same objective – machines delivered and installed without any delays or damage. A problem-solving process can be used for this issue, within the context of the total negotiation, which may involve many other variables – specifications, cost, service, warranties, installation, training, etc.

A simple six-step model for solving problems is illustrated in Figure 5.

You will find this process useful as you prepare for your negotiations, as more complex situations invariably have more issues to be resolved. If you are skilled in using the process you will also find yourself becoming the natural lead within a negotiation when joint problem-solving is needed.

The You Try It section following has a simple problem-solving situation for you to test your new skills on.

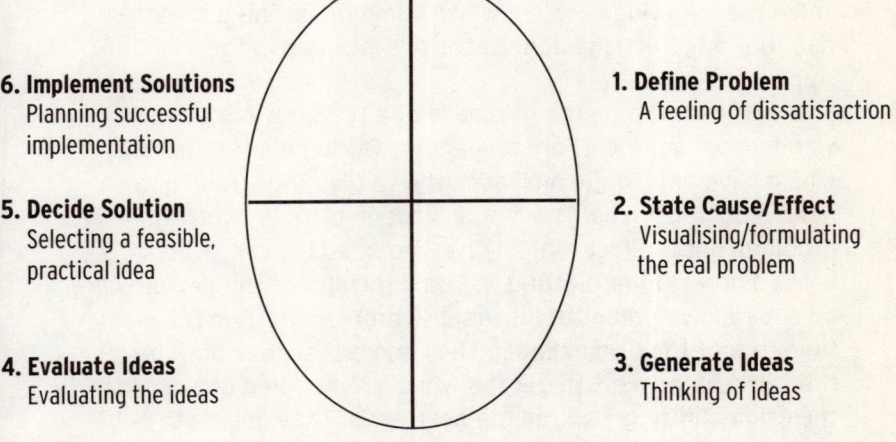

Problem-solving: A right brain–left brain activity

Figure 5: A six-step problem-solving model   Courtesy Priority Ma

Creativity – building the best deal

Key Point Summary
- Part of our brain is adept at creative thinking
- Creativity is a process and skill that can be developed
- Creative approaches expand the content of the negotiation
- Creative thinking supporting analytical thinking is the best way to develop a win/win approach by both parties
- Creative approaches and processes applied within a negotiation will significantly enhance a win/win outcome
- Brainstorming and mind-mapping are two simple and effective creative activities that can be used at all stages of a negotiation
- Negotiation involves two or more parties, each with different objectives, seeking to reach agreement
- Problem-solving involves two or more parties, each with the same objective, seeking the best solution
- Problem-solving may occur within a negotiation
- Problem-solving involves a six-step process

▶ YOU TRY IT

Your opportunity to apply some creative thinking to a problem! Using the six-step process, how might you manage to solve the following problem which came up during a recent negotiation? (A suggested scenario is included in the Appendix.)

Sue is negotiating the purchase of a two-year-old station wagon from her local Ford dealership. During her discussions, which have been quite amicable, the value of her trade-in has been a point of issue. The actual trade-in price is not the problem, but the fact that she has modified the rear wheels using a non-standard fitting is. The difficulty for the dealer will be a very low number of buyers; the problem for Sue is lack of time to refit the original gear. They agree that they both have the same objective – to get the wheels remodified or revert to the original fitting – within the next week. They decide to put their problem-solving hats on, using the six-step problem-solving model!

3 | Structure and process

▶Negotiation is by nature both strategic and tactical. Strategy involves taking a big-picture and often long-term view; tactics involve the detailed steps and actions to achieve the strategic objectives. Strategy for a negotiation involves structure; tactics are often process driven. Good negotiators are both strategic and tactical, and they achieve this by 'getting their head around' the structure and the process. Negotiation invariably involves 'selling' – ideas, propositions, ourselves.

Stage by stage... the strategic view

When an eagle's soaring at 3000 feet, it has its total territory in view. In business terms it's the big picture. Negotiators have to be like eagles – up above the crowd, seeing the boundaries, searching for predators and prey alike, locating the hot spots of activity, deciding on attack and retreat areas, looking for problem spots and points of opportunity. Failure to be a strategist first invariably results in getting an inferior outcome. The eagle does not view inferior results as acceptable – neither does a good negotiator.

> **An eagle's strategic view of negotiation. First, it has a structure. Second, it is a process. The process works within the structure.**

Figure 6 (p. 38) illustrates the structure. We use a five-stage format.

Let's illustrate the structure from a strategic view, using a simple personal negotiation situation.

An old wire fence forms the boundary with your neighbour.

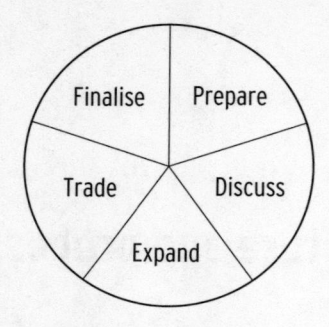

Figure 6: The negotiation structure

They've indicated they'd like to repair it, which basically involves some new posts and a top and bottom wire. You, however, would prefer it removed, and a new paling fence erected. A classic negotiation situation – same deal but different objectives.

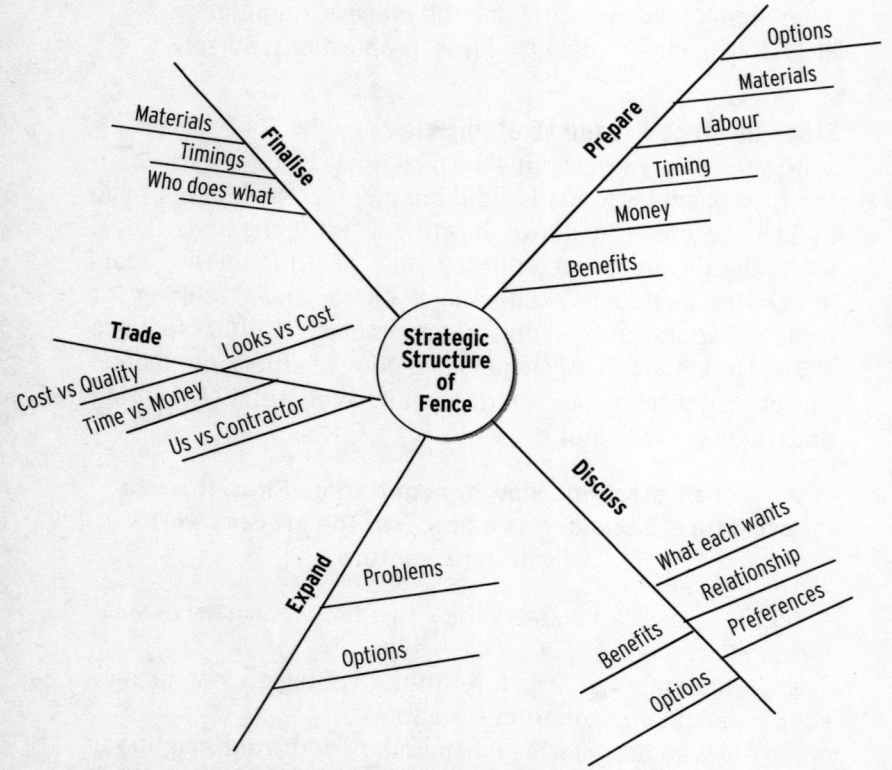

Figure 7: Strategic stucture of fence negotiation

38 | Negotiation Skills

Taking the eagle view, the strategist studies the situation as a negotiation structure.

Prepare: Homework on other fences locally; aesthetics of other constructions; cost factors; neighbour's financial situation, occupation, hobbies; other boundaries; garden; value increase.
Discuss: Where?; when?; who's involved?; tone; emotions; neighbour's real needs and wants.
Expand: Suggest options; explore alternatives; solve problems.
Trade: Give and take areas; bottom-lines.
Finalise: Commitment; mutual satisfaction; action plan; responsibilities; implement.

Figure 7 (p. 38) shows this as a mind-map. This is your strategic view of the structure of this negotiation – the eagle's view from on high!

A business situation is no different. Your company has a contract to supply engineering parts to a manufacturer in China. You are responsible for negotiating the delivery contract with the East Asia Shipping Company.

Taking the strategist's view on the structure of the negotiation, complete the mind map below.

Figure 8a: Stategic structure of delivery negotiation

Structure and process | 39

How does it compare with Figure 8b? Did you put too much detail? Remember at this point we are looking at the big picture, seeing the whole containing the parts. We can go into the parts and flesh out the detail when we look at the process. We then become tacticians – the eagle swooping, all senses working!

Strategic Structure of China Delivery

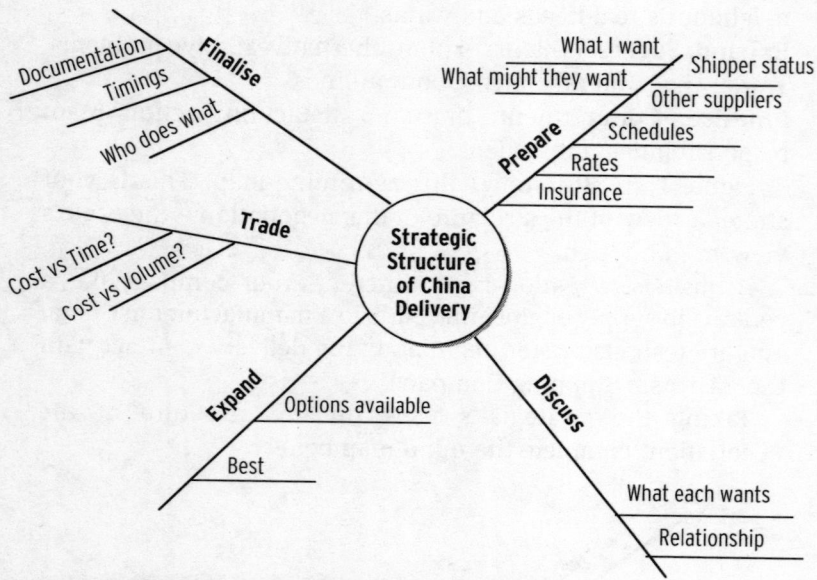

- **Finalise**: Documentation, Timings, Who does what
- **Prepare**: What I want, What might they want, Shipper status, Other suppliers, Schedules, Rates, Insurance
- **Trade**: Cost vs Time?, Cost vs Volume?
- **Expand**: Options available, Best
- **Discuss**: What each wants, Relationship

Figure 8b: Stategic structure of delivery negotiation

Now that you understand the structure of a negotiation, and how to take the strategic view, let's move to the tactical aspects.

Step by step . . . the tactical view

The tactician is involved in the detail of getting to the destination. The tactician must understand each part of the journey – the process of getting from point to point, each step relying on achievement of the preceding step. A failure at one step may mean the journey is not completed, or not completed in some way – over time, over budget, partial outcome only, parties unhappy, etc.

So the tactical negotiator is interested in every step of the negotiation process. Some can be preplanned and prepared for. At many times during the journey, however, the tactician will be confronted by unplanned and unexpected events. If they have done their planning fully, using the 'What if . . .' method, they will have contingency plans and actions available to them.

So let's look at the step-by-step process of a simple negotiation from the tactical view.

Figure 9: Simple negotiation model – structure and process

Using either the personal (boundary fence) or business (delivery contract) negotiation situation, complete the process details on the blank mind-map on page 42. Use the one already completed – just add the process details. For example, 'relative importance of each variable' in the Fence Negotiation is covered by expanding Money, Labour, Options, Materials and adding 'What might each party really want?' Just include everything you can think of under each of the tactical steps. Then compare it with the suggested mind-maps in Figures 10 and 11. You will see how the strategic mind-map has been expanded to include the tactical view.

How did you go? Yours will be different from the one suggested – after all, negotiation is both an art and a science,

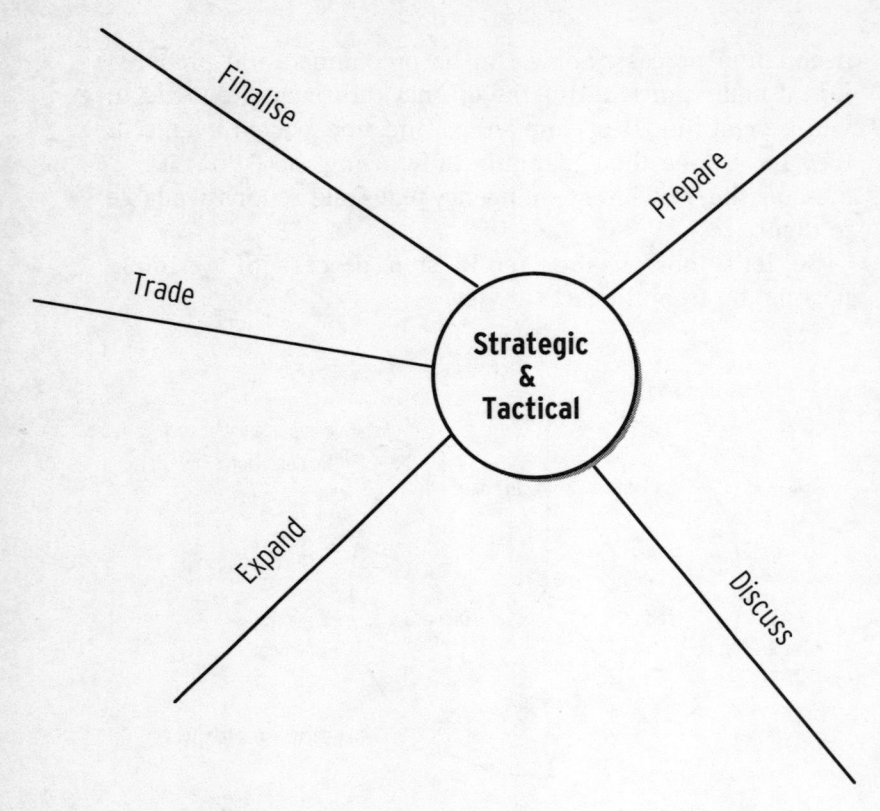

```
         Finalise              Prepare

  Trade          ┌─────────┐
                 │Strategic│
                 │    &    │
                 │Tactical │
                 └─────────┘
         Expand              Discuss
```

so the parameters are not fixed. In fact, whereas a journey should always end up at the planned destination, a negotiation rarely does. Where it does end up is largely determined by the extent and quality of your preparation and your skills as a negotiator. The outcome may be far better than you expected, or far worse. But research shows that two good negotiators will achieve more of a win/win than mismatched negotiators, who tend to end up with a skewed win/lose outcome – and the extent of that 'win' is more often than not less than the matched-skills negotiation.

> If I had nine hours to cut down a tree, I would spend six hours sharpening my axe!
> **Abraham Lincoln**

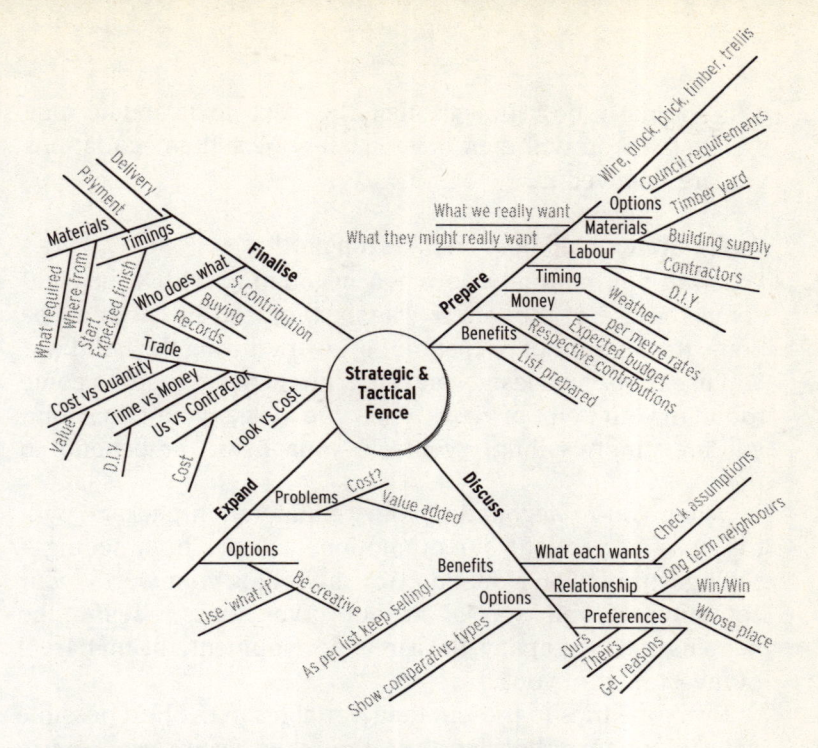

Figure 10: Strategic and tactical fence negotiation

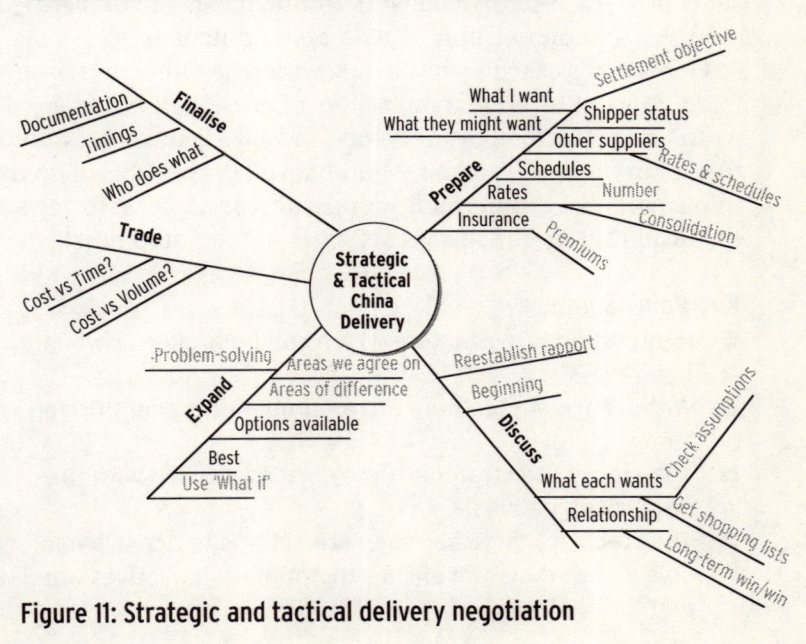

Figure 11: Strategic and tactical delivery negotiation

Structure and process | 43

In summary, be a strategist first, then dive down and become a tactician. You will then have mastery over the negotiations you are involved in.

You're always selling . . . don't stop now!

What do you naturally do when negotiating with your child about the use of the family wagon, the need for study to be done, the amount of pocket money, work during the holidays? You use every persuasive tactic you know to get them to come round to your point of view. When you look at your behaviour, you are simply selling – yourself, your ideas, the benefits to them.

When you're negotiating your remuneration package with the boss as part of your promotion, you are both selling – selling within the negotiation. You are selling your worth, your commitment, your special attributes; your boss is selling the benefits of the company, the career development, the high level of investment in you.

Everyone tries to present their variables in the best possible light to enhance their worth in the other party's eyes and to show how the benefits will work for them. And all to increase their negotiation position to get a better outcome.

Fine – that's exactly what selling within negotiation is meant to do. Most of us are natural sellers of ourselves, but many of us freeze at the thought of having to 'sell'. You cannot afford that luxury in a negotiation. Mind-map all the benefits of doing things your way and you'll go in with confidence. To repeat the heading – you're always selling . . . don't stop now!

Key Point Summary

- Negotiation is a structure which can be broken down into five stages
- Within each stage, there are a number of process-driven steps
- The stages are strategic – they are concerned with the primary objectives
- The steps are tactical – they are actions to achieve mini-objectives which will ensure the primary objectives are met

- There is a logical order to the steps of the process
- Best outcomes are achieved by following the process
- Using creative thinking activities for various steps of the process will enhance the outcome
- Selling within negotiation is a normal and necessary activity

> If you have built castles in the air,
> your work need not be lost;
> that is where they should be.
> Now put the foundations under them.
> **Henry David Thoreau**

4 | You are in a negotiation - why?

▶Negotiations are an integral part of living. Many of our transactions involve the process of negotiation. Future events are moulded by our current transactions – both outcomes and behaviours. The extent and quality of our preparation for a negotiation always affects the outcome. We have total control over the preparation stage of a negotiation. We must be very clear about the reason we are negotiating. When we have completed our preparation we should have clear written objectives.

Getting what we want . . . and they what they want

Life sometimes seems like one big transaction. We spend our waking time involved in satisfying our needs and wants, and others' needs and wants, to pass the time from birth to death. Cynical? Perhaps, but when we look closely at what we do every day, every week, every year, we are essentially involved in a series of transactions. To be sure, the vast majority of them are simple and repetitive and require no great mental or physical effort on our part. Some, however, are significant, in that their outcome affects subsequent patterns.

We are not concerned with the repetitive small transactions – the boys will mow the lawn each week in return for the car on Saturday; I'll very happily do the weekly ironing in exchange for my wife doing the personal accounts. Those trades were negotiated many months or years ago and remain in place because they continue to work for our family unit.

What we are concerned with are those transactions that involve us with others in situations where objectives differ and the eventual outcomes affect future relationships and events. They are likely to be irregular in nature, although many business transactions are negotiated on a prescheduled basis.

So a negotiation is a transaction between two or more parties, each of whom has a different objective, where they exchange items of value called variables in order to reach agreement. It may or may not be mutually satisfying, either as a process or in outcome. But the fact remains that the two parties need each other, or would like to have a relationship. Spouses, partners, buyer-seller, leader-follower, manager-staff, employer-employee, contractor-subcontractor, doctor-patient, wholesaler-retailer – we all form relationships to get what we want. And to make these relationships work for us, and the other party, we are likely to find ourselves in a negotiation with them.

As you have already done some strategic thinking about the boundary fence and the delivery contract, let's use those as we focus on the tactical aspects of the negotiation process. But first we'll explore the Background Step of the Preparation stage of our negotiation model, which will help us focus on the detail as tacticians.

Figure 12: Preparation – background

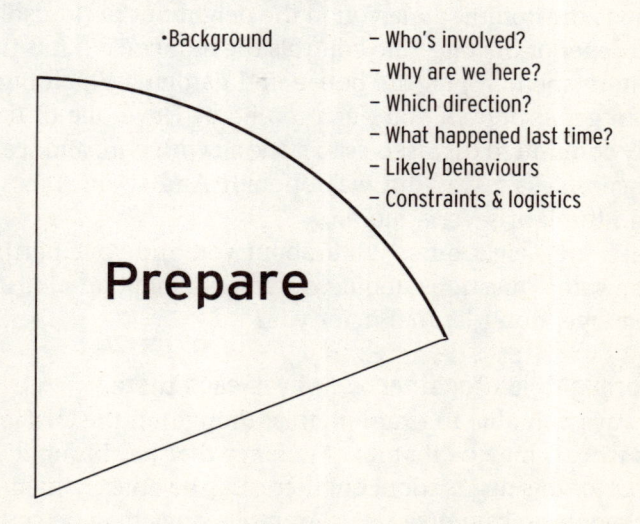

- Background
  - Who's involved?
  - Why are we here?
  - Which direction?
  - What happened last time?
  - Likely behaviours
  - Constraints & logistics

Prepare

You can see there are some background facts we need to know before we are in a position to start detailed preparation.

That's not to say discussions won't have taken place – in most cases they will have. You and your neighbour will have broached the subject of the wire fence needing replacing, and you may already have an existing shipping arrangement with East Asia Shipping, and deal with them regularly. But it is important that you treat the new negotiation as new – after all, circumstances do change, and to cling to past methods or solutions may now be inappropriate. So let's follow the process, understand why we do it, and fill in some of the details.

Who's involved ... positions, politics, personalities and power?

We must know who we are going to negotiate with. Your neighbour is not one person, but two if they're a couple, and maybe even three or four if teenagers are on site. Each have their own preferences, values, feelings and opinions. So do you. And if your partner is involved, you could have four or more parties to the negotiation. The complexities increase exponentially! Let's keep it simple – two couples, good long-term relationship as neighbours, they want wire repaired, you want new paling.

Who is the dominant person in the neighbour partnership – the gardener or the one who controls the money? What is their attitude to spending on the house and garden? Which one is likely to get stroppy if you push too hard? Have one of them already committed themselves to sticking with wire and would lose face unless a way out was offered? And so on. I'm sure you can think of several more.

That's the neighbours. What about you and your partner? Ask the same questions about yourselves. Some home truths may emerge, don't let that deter you!

What brought you together ... why is each there?

It's always valuable to examine this, though on the surface it seems trite. It may be that it is the fence that has brought you together for this negotiation, but there may be other, sometimes unspoken, issues involved. For example, dogs may be getting through the broken wire, and the gardener is annoyed that the flower beds are ruined. Or maybe friends of yours have made less than complimentary comments about 'that messy ugly fence' and your pride is hurt. So don't accept the reason you are together at face value – have a deeper look.

Which direction... converging or diverging?
If you are both converging, the negotiation is likely to be more collaborative. Remember, if you're in total agreement on the objective, then it is not a negotiation, but a problem-solving situation. Use the problem-solving model covered in Chapter 2.

If you are diverging, you need to think about where the differences are, how far apart you are, and why the gap is getting bigger. Maybe it is cost. Maybe it is because they are thinking of selling, but haven't told you yet. Or perhaps they have already bought the replacement wire and some mesh and are too embarrassed to admit it – particularly as you have indicated you'd prefer paling!

Déjà vu... or what happened last time?
History does give a fair and reasonable view of likely future events. Having said that, you will be able to recall many negotiations where history was turned upside down, and the nature and outcome of a negotiation was virtually the opposite of what you expected.

So look closely at what happened last time as a guide. Are the circumstances the same or similar? What's the financial situation and climate? Are the same people involved? Was the outcome of the previous negotiation satisfying to them? If so, are they likely to favour a repeat? When we last met, the negotiation was about something entirely different; is that outcome going to work for or against us this time?

Behaviours... 95% habitual!
In Chapter 1 we talked about our predictability, based on the fact that our behaviour is about 95% habitual. So if we know who we are dealing with, and the nature of the negotiation is similar to previous ones, we can make a reasonable assumption that their behaviour will not have significantly changed. Now note the word assumption. They may have changed, or been told to change, or been told or decided to modify their usual

behaviour – which could throw you if you placed heavy reliance on them not changing.

What about your own behaviour? Does your predictability make you vulnerable? Perhaps you could modify aspects which cause others to become offensive or defensive. Or by considering the outcome you want, and the nature of the other party, you could adopt a particular style for that particular negotiation.

Returning to the neighbour and fence negotiation, is there a pattern that you can rely on? If one of them talks incessantly, then use that to gather information. If one is reticent, then have some questions prepared to draw out their opinions and feelings. If one likes to make decisions quickly, have the coffee pot ready to slow them down. Negotiation is all about managing situations and people and emotions – not just tangible things!

Constraints . . . managing the logistics
The logistics are the most simple things to arrange, but in our experience they are far too often left to chance. The result is that these small matters become major issues and cloud the real issues and purpose of the negotiation. Let's look at some common examples.

The meeting room size is too small; no refreshments have been organised; the negotiation goes through lunch with no food; the meeting room is booked for two hours when the negotiation is expected to last four; one of the lead negotiators has to leave early with no warning given; documents essential for reviewing before agreement can be reached are not available, and so on. I'm sure you have experienced a number, if not all, of these at some stage in your negotiations.

So, before you get the neighbours over to discuss the fence, get the room ready, the coffee out, make sure you have milk and sugar, and if you're optimistic about the outcome have a bottle in the fridge. And tell the kids to stay outside, and switch on the answerphone!

> Assumption is the mother of screw up.
> **Angelo Donghia**

Let's recap by focusing on the delivery contract.

Who's involved? Individual or team? Position in the shipping company? Given that, what power do they have? Do they have the final authority? If not who does? Should they be involved? Should I take one of my team? What could they contribute? Would that enhance or diminish my perceived authority?

What brought you together? Is this contract one of several similar ones? Is there a preferred shipper arrangement? Can we get competitive quotes as leverage? Can we go to a competitor for this contract? Do they already have contracts with us for China? Can we merge consignments?

Which direction? Are we working more closely recently in terms of costs, insurance, documentation, damages, packaging, pick-up, delivery method, credit, etc? Or is the overall relationship deteriorating, and if so, why?

What happened last time? Were the circumstances similar? What was the same? What was different? Did we achieve our objectives in terms of cost, documentation, insurance, etc? Were they amenable to our suggestions and requests? Has the arrangement worked for both parties?

Behaviours: What negotiating behaviours do they usually adopt? Are they likely to change? Are we comfortable with their style? Do we need to change ours to enhance the outcome? If so, what do we need to do?

Constraints: How quickly does this contract have to be in place? Where should the negotiation meeting take place? Who should be there from our team? How long will it take? Room availability and booking? Refreshment arrangements? Time constraints on them? Legal documentation available? Contract documents available? Shipping schedules and estimates printed and available? Authorities signed off?

Seems like lots of questions, but in negotiation sure is always better than sorry!

Key Point Summary
- Negotiation occurs because we have to manage transactions where objectives differ
- Essentially, negotiations have the objective of 'getting what we want'. Win/win approaches add 'while they get what they want'
- The preparation for any negotiation involves research – quantity and quality
- Attitudes and behaviours – of both parties – must be factored in
- The better the preparation, the better the outcome

▶ **YOU TRY IT**
The checklist opposite will assess how well you prepare for a negotiation. (Comments are included in the Appendix.)

During preparation	Almost always	Often	Some-times	Seldom	Almost never
1. I focus on the person I think will be the main negotiator					
2. I work out what I want to achieve first, then their possible needs					
3. I use my notes from previous negotiations to decide what they might want					
4. I use mind-maps or other creative tools for scenario setting					
5. I consider the likely politics					
6. I assume that their initial approach may be flexible					
7. I consider our past relationship					
8. I consider our current relationship					
9. I think about the end result I want in material and emotional terms					
10. I write all my calculations down					
11. I work out a contingency plan for each aspect					
12. I calculate a best, likely and worst outcome for me					
13. I consider the effect on the relationship if we don't manage to agree					
14. I take into account the timing factors for them					
15. I work out how I will handle them if they get tough					
16. I involve others as a sounding-board					
17. I plan to use a similar approach to the last time if it worked well					
18. I take their feelings into account during my planning					
19. I prepare the legal paperwork on the assumption we will agree					
20. I work on the basis that both parties desire a win/win outcome					
Total ✓	×5	×4	×3	×2	×1
Total/100					

5 | Outcomes

▶The end result of a negotiation is an outcome. We set our objectives in terms of a desired or acceptable outcome. There are six possible outcomes, with varied levels of win, lose, and no deal. Each outcome has consequences for both parties. Relationships are affected. Emotional outcomes are as important as material outcomes. Approaches, styles and behaviours affect the negotiation and the outcome.

Now that we have prepared the background to our negotiation, we need to understand the range of outcomes possible. We've already discussed the extremes of behaviour which result in skewed outcomes. We now need to look at all six.

At the end of the day . . . there are only six

Outcomes are expressed in terms of win and lose, or no deal.

Win/lose: This is the overly competitive stance. It says there is a fixed amount available, and I will take as much of it as I can get, and I will try to get it all. I will work to make sure you don't get any.

'I'll get what I want. You won't get what you want.'

Lose/win: This is the overly collaborative outcome. It knows that the amount can be shared, but in order to appease the other party – or just to get a deal – is prepared to give most, if not all of the variables away.

'You will get what you want. I won't get what I want.'

Lose/lose: This usually occurs between two competitive parties. Neither is willing to concede, often through fear of losing more.

They do, however, need each other and come to an agreement, even though it is distasteful for them both. Typically lose/lose is the result of scarcity thinking and a lack of creativity. Past experience of losing is also a strong influence.

'Neither of us will get what we want.'

No-deal: This outcome is often preferable to any of the above. We'll consider consequences of all the outcomes shortly. Suffice to say that if the outcome is beyond your preplanned bottom line, then you are better to walk away. It is not a sign of weakness – indeed it usually indicates a well-prepared negotiation position that would work towards a win/win if that were possible.

'If we can't find a way that benefits us both let's agree to disagree. Maybe we can find a better way in the future.'

Win: This is an outcome we use quite often, perhaps thinking that we are working towards a win/win. There is a major difference. The win outcome is desired by the negotiator who says I am looking after my own interests and I will be working towards getting what I want. However, I am quite happy for you to look after your own side and win too – there is probably plenty to go around. I won't be trying to do you down, as whether you win or lose is immaterial to me.

'I'll get what I want and leave you to get what you want.'

Win/win: This is an active approach by both parties to see if both can achieve most, if not all, of what each wants. It comes from an abundance mentality which says there is enough to go around, and we should search together to see if there's any more. It is essentially a collaborative approach with a high degree of creativity from both parties.

'Let's look for a way that will get us each what we want.'

It's worth having a look at the consequences of each of these outcomes.

A win/lose is OK if there is no ongoing relationship. As long as the party who 'lost' completes their side of the deal, the 'winner' gets what they wanted. Where there is an ongoing relationship, however, the consequences are negative to both. The outcome will influence future negotiations, as the 'loser' takes steps to ensure it never happens again. There is always the opportunity for the 'loser' to claw back what has been lost, subtly or openly. This may involve deliberate delays, service defects, late documentation, cost overruns, go-slows, etc – the ways to claw back are only limited by the imagination! And in the next negotiation the 'loser' will adopt a competitive stance that may well wipe out the extra gains the 'winner' made from the first deal.

A lose/win is equally bad for both. Initially it could cause losses for the 'loser' which may affect their ability or willingness to do business with the 'winner', meaning a real loss for both. They may have to renege on some aspects. Similar to the win/lose, the subsequent events are likely to impact negatively on the relationship.

A lose/lose is bad for both. Sometimes, such as in a renegotiation of a contract for continuity, both parties would prefer to walk away, but can't. So their aim will be to limit the losses to both parties – which could possibly be viewed as a very low level win/win! However, where the lose/lose is a result of both parties taking an uncompromising stance, the consequences are totally negative. Frustration, personality clashes, withdrawal, delays, non-compliance and non-completion are common.

A no-deal may have negative consequences in that both parties are free to take their business elsewhere. That may mean the end of the relationship, at least in the short term. However, given the negative consequences of the outcomes above, it is often regarded in hindsight as the most suitable outcome at that time. Circumstances change, and providing the personal relationships were kept positive, it is likely that the next negotiation will have a positive result.

A win is an interesting one. If both parties are aware that they are individually responsible for looking after their own interests, then a win/win will result. The question remains, of course, as to whether they might have got a better result if they had adopted a win/win in the first place! What usually happens is that shared creativity is stifled and alternative ways of doing the deal don't occur.

A win/win is the preferred outcome where an ongoing

relationship is necessary. Thus, all family, personal, social, professional and business negotiations should aim for a win/win. That does not mean you can't get tough! It does not mean you can't be a bit soft! But whether you are tough or soft, you have built it into your tactical plan. Nothing is donated! A win/win means that both parties are happy with the outcome, will work hard to make it work as planned, and will do business with each other again in the future.

Whatever the outcome, there are some common consequences:
- We personally have to live with it
- Our associates – partners, family, friends or colleagues – have to live with it
- Our companies have to live with it
- It shapes the nature of the relationship
- It influences the way we do business together in the future
- It influences the next negotiation
- It sets precedents for many parties

So careful thinking about the consequences of any outcome is a vital part of your preparation, and the mark of a good negotiator.

A win squared ... can 3 + 3 = 9?

'Synergy' is a term used in business to justify a merger. A few mergers produce more than the sum of their parts, but history records that most do not. So are we way over the top when we suggest that outcomes can be win-squared? Experience from our graduates over the years indicates they often achieve synergy – the win that both parties achieved was greater than either expected, each ending up with more. The zero-sum players would no doubt disagree, but let's have a look at a couple of typical examples that we've had reported to us.

An appliance manufacturer shipped its cartons singly, in bulk and in full pallets. It split its freighting between rail and truck: full pallets went by rail; single and bulk by truck. The truck freighting company gave the manufacturer the full pallet rate for everything it freighted, which was the cheapest for the manufacturer. This meant the truck company was losing 'cream' to rail. The manufacturer had recently imported some new products for distribution throughout the country and approached the truck company for a quote. The negotiation that followed resulted in an expanded and more flexible pick-up and distribution service by the truck company, who delivered full pallets to the rail head, consolidated the bulk into containers, introduced a computerised consignment-note printer for the manufacturer, and organised single and small deliveries through its associate courier company. Each party considered the outcome better than they had thought possible: rail kept its business which was under threat; the trucking company increased its share through the extra product being shipped, made more margin by consolidating, strengthened its relationship with the manufacturer by providing a dedicated consignment-note printer, and kept the single deliveries within its group. The manufacturer ended up with the trucking company taking the complete distribution off their hands, getting a new record system at no cost, improving their service to both large and small retailers, and reducing the delivery cost per carton. A real win squared!

Bruce was interested in a special-offer guitar and amplifier deal. The guitar was excellent but the amplifier did not have the reverb unit which he particularly required. The special offer price was within his budget, but to upgrade the amplifier was not, and the dealer couldn't include a better one in the special offer deal. They discussed it for a few minutes, but neither could see a way around the seemingly fixed components of the deal. Then the dealer said: 'Give me an hour.' The dealer phoned two amplifier importers that he sourced from, and located a repossessed amplifier which had everything Bruce wanted, in as-new condition, at a price below the lesser specified amplifier in the special offer. So when Bruce returned to what he thought would be to continue the negotiation based on price, he found a deal tailor-made for him – guitar, superb amplifier, and all at the special-offer price with full warranties on both. And the dealer gained a customer who would highly recommend him to his musical friends, reinforced his reputation with the importer and, of course, made another profitable sale. Bruce thinks he got a brilliant deal! So does the dealer!

I always start a negotiation session off by giving each group

of five or six business people an orange and a knife. I then ask them to see if everyone can get what they want from the orange. They can assume any identity they like. A few years ago most groups would end up cutting the orange into equal segments, reflecting the prevailing thinking at that time. 'We're willing to share, so let's share it evenly.' Now you would rarely find a group doing that – they come up with a whole range of interesting possibilities. Typically they adopt some unusual roles. For example:
- Kelly is a photographer – she'll use it tonight in a shoot
- Peter is a juggler – he'll use it in his kid's show tomorrow
- Rebecca is a cook – on Friday she'll use the peel for icing, the pulp for the cake, and her mother will drink the juice!

The point of the exercise is not lost on them. The orange stays on their group table throughout the seminar and it never gets eaten. During discussions, the win-squared nature of the outcome keeps coming up, and people remember the simple lessons. Ask questions to check needs and wants. Don't assume – be creative, expand options, exchange.

> Help other people get what they want – and you'll get what you want. **Mary Kay Ash**

Your approach is critical . . . it shapes the outcome
We have covered the competitive/collaborative continuum and looked at the consequences of behaviours. We have also covered the assertion model and the benefits of being assertive. Figure 13 (p. 60) outlines the approaches taken on various aspects of a negotiation by Aggressives (win/lose); Assertives (win/win); Passives (lose/win). Where do you currently fit?

Problems not people . . . interests not positions
Old habits die hard, and many of us still get caught up in the emotional aspects of a negotiation. It's quite hard to remain objective all the time and keep your feelings under control when people and personalities and the issues provoke strong reactions within you. Alas, you must!

AGGRESSIVE	**ASSERTIVE**	**PASSIVE**
Win/Lose Approach	Win/Win Approach	Lose/Win Approach
I'll get my way; you won't get yours	Let's find a better way; not your way, not my way	You'll probably get your way; I won't get mine
You are my adversary	We are problem solvers	You are my friend
I distrust you	We'll proceed independent of trust	I trust you
My objective is victory and I'll apply pressure to achieve it	Our objective is an effective and amicable outcome and we'll reason and be open to reason to achieve it	My objective is agreement and I'll yield to pressure to achieve it
I must get concessions from you	The best solutions don't depend on concessions	I must offer concessions to you
It's good to be confrontational	We'll confront the problem, not each other	It's good to be conciliatory
I'll take a position	Let's focus on the reasons behind our positions	I'll change my position easily
I'll make threats	We'll explore interests	I'll make offers
I'll mislead you about my bottom line	We'll avoid bottom lines	I'll disclose my bottom line
I'll search for an answer I can accept	Let's develop options to choose between	I'll search for an answer you can accept
I'll insist on my position	Let's insist on agreement	I'll insist on agreement

Courtesy Priority Management

Figure 13: Competitive-collaborative approaches

The rules are simple – focus on the problems, not the people behind the problem. Focus on their interests, not the position they are adopting. Experience shows that we can deal quite well with problems and interests, and involve our normal emotions when discussing them, providing we separate them from the initiators.

Your business peer criticises your department's decision on computer software, which you can handle, but then begins to [attack] one of your analysts. You interrupt with: 'You may [have a v]alid point about the decision, but Craig's personal life has nothing to do with the issue we're negotiating. I suggest we leave personalities out of this and focus on the real problem for both of us – getting the best networking system in place before the end of the year.' It is a real skill, but one you should master if you are involved in regular and major negotiations.

Material wins . . . emotional wins

Our competitive environment shapes our attitudes to a win being based on material outcomes. We talk about success in material terms. We base our education system on material outcomes. We base our self-esteem on what we have achieved in material things. We judge others by their material achievements in money and tangibles. Whether you accept materialism as good or bad is immaterial – the simple fact is that we pay too little attention to the emotional aspects of people and situations. This is a pity, because people respond very positively to emotional satisfactions – humans are emotional creatures first and foremost!

In negotiation, emotional aspects are very important. We estimate that over half of a person's assessment of success or failure in a negotiation is based on how they feel. In case-study exercises, we ask groups to assess their material and emotional outcomes. We get them to assess their emotional outcomes during the negotiation, immediately it is concluded, after debriefing within their group, and after a total class debrief. More discussion is generated by the assessment of emotional outcomes than the material result! People basically want to be treated fairly and reasonably, and if they feel they have been poorly treated (colloquially done-down, screwed, ripped off, patronised, etc) they will react as if it were a lose/win outcome. This reaction will be regardless of the material outcome they achieved. It may have been an extremely profitable result, but the feelings will colour the real outcome.

One of the most common areas where we see this apply – and many of us will relate to – is buying and selling a house, a car, or anything of reasonable value to us. Most of us will recall the feelings after the deal had been done – was it a fair deal, did I get enough for it, was I too soft, perhaps I shouldn't have taken their first offer, etc. If the other party acted professionally, gave a little, made you feel that the deal was fair, you were quite happy. In fact, you probably bragged a bit about the 'good deal I did on my car'! Even if you had hoped to get more, or pay less, you will always be able to justify the material outcome – but it's the emotional outcome you have to live with.

The lesson for negotiators: if you look after the emotional outcome of the other party you may well have to give less in material terms.

A few weeks ago I had to buy a new camcorder for our presentation skills seminar – we video our students as they practise. The model we need is not available in every electronic appliance retailer, as it has to take a full-sized video cassette tape. The salesperson, Les, was particularly helpful and managed to locate one for me. We then discussed price, terms, a tripod, tapes, credit card versus a cheque, and we negotiated a fair deal. I felt pretty good, and I knew I could justify the account to Ruth, our very strict financial controller. But then Les made me feel very good – he made sure I had everything I needed, checked that all the bits were in place and worked, helped me through a demonstration take, and gave me tips on focusing and zooming. He then swapped the tapes for better ones, arranged for an extra-long cord to be made up, and personally delivered everything to our seminar centre on his way home! I can tell you that I not only felt good about the material outcome, but pretty spoiled as a relatively small customer. No doubt Les was very happy with the deal too – but it was me who was emotionally satisfied!

Key Point Summary
- Our preparation must include our desired outcome
- The best outcome is a win/win, as we are likely to achieve more of what we want
- A loss should be avoided – a no deal may be preferable
- A creative approach may result in a win squared outcome – where the total results of both parties exceeded their individual expectations

- There are always consequences of any outcome – we have to live with them
- We should focus on the problems, not the people
- We should focus on the issues and interests, not the positions people take
- Emotional outcomes are often more important than material outcomes – we must look after their feelings

▶ YOU TRY IT

Based on Figure 13, write a phrase that you could use in each of the following negotiation situations as a win/win assertive approach. (Some examples are included in the Appendix.)

1. Partner upset with holiday arrangements
2. Parent opposed to allowance request
3. Grandparent insisting on holiday visit
4. Council charging for street lighting upgrade
5. Colleague objecting to your space request
6. Supplier insisting on extra quality checks
7. Retailer charging for delivery outside free area
8. Boss imposing tasks beyond job requirements
9. Staff member with unreasonable expectations
10. Neighbour with obnoxious noisy teenagers

6 | The gaps – analysing the tension for change

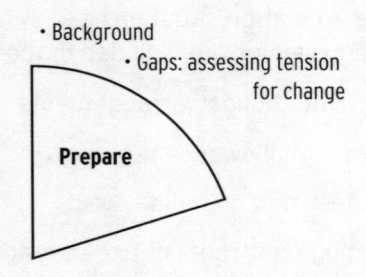

- Background
- Gaps: assessing tension for change

Prepare

▶ The reason for a negotiation is a gap between what each party has now and what they would like to have. The gap between the current reality and the desired result creates a tension – a tension for change. The size and urgency of the gap affects the strength of the tension for change. The relative strengths directly affect each party's approach and can strongly influence the conduct of the negotiation. To avoid being locked in, we should have a BATNA – an alternative to a loss outcome.

How wide is the gap . . . how strong is the pull?

When we want something urgently, the desire to get it is strong. We will take all the necessary steps to get it quickly. We may even sacrifice our normal standards, or pay more for it. Similarly, when something is important to us, we adjust our behaviour to ensure we get what we want.

> **The difference between what we have now and what we want is called a gap. The size or extent of that gap or difference causes tension for change.**

If the gap is small, the tension for change will be low. For example, last season I bought a new tennis racquet. I see that a better model has just been released. I'd quite like to change, but there's nothing wrong with my existing one. It's still almost new, will last another two seasons, and I really can't justify the extravagance. The difference between what I have now and what I'd like is really quite small, certainly neither urgent nor important, and it would take some super salesperson to convince me that I should change.

But what if my existing racquet was three years old, a bit tired, with a grip that really didn't suit me any longer, and was heavier than the latest model? Would the gap between the new and old be large? Would I want it soon? Yes to both! The gap is wide, the tension for change high. Urgent and important to me. It would not even require a salesperson to convince me – I've convinced myself!

Why is knowledge about both parties' gaps and respective tensions for change important to negotiators? Because they have a fundamental impact on the content of the negotiation, and the outcome. Let's look at a personal situation most of us find ourselves in at some stage of our homeowning lives.

The need for a bigger house has been growing for a few months; perhaps the family numbers have increased, or they have got older, or extended family have moved in permanently, or business dictates an extra room as a study. You haven't listed your house but recently had an agent give you an idea of its value. So you've gone to a few open homes and followed up some leads, an activity you have called 'just looking'! But then yesterday you saw the perfect house: location, size, setting, number of rooms, layout and even the study were tailor-made for you! Do you want it? Yes! Do you want to do something about it urgently? Yes, I don't want to miss out! Is it important to you? Yes, very – it's perfect for the rest of my life!

Now, there's a buyer out there somewhere for your existing house. Do you want them to look at yours quickly? To make a quick decision? To give you an unconditional deal so you can make sure your offer on your dream home is accepted above all others? Yes to those three! Are you prepared to accept a lower than indicated price for a quick sale? Well, I suppose so

> There is only one way under high heaven to get anybody to do anything. And that is by making the other person want to do it.
> **Dale Carnegie**

– maybe. And there's the rub. Is the gap between the existing and potential new situation urgent and important enough for you to give up money for? Again, maybe. And that decision may well involve changed values.

If the value of moving and living in the dream home is high, it may well outweigh the cost of selling quickly, even though your normal pattern of spending is conservative. We do change our value systems when circumstances dictate!

The point of the exercise is that in a negotiation it is obviously of great value to you if you know the other party's gaps and tension for change. Where are they now versus where they would like to be after the negotiation? How much do they want from this negotiation? How badly do they want what we are offering? We can check these out by assessing their tension for change.

Assessing tension for change . . . the key is the quotient

We designed a form to assess both parties' tension for change, and our graduates find it extremely useful for even minor negotiations. See Figure 14.

The example that we've used is typical of the ones we receive from our graduates as they give us feedback on how they are managing negotiations in their business environment. You will see that the supplier would very much like to secure this business as the potential customer is large, has the opportunity to grow, has potential for cross-selling other products and services, and could become a major account. Thus their tension for change, on a scale of 1 (low) to 10 (high), is about 8.

What does that mean? In simple terms, they are strongly motivated to get a deal. For a negotiator, this sends warning signals! If I'm that keen to get a deal, I may be tempted to give things away; I may trade my variables too cheaply. I need to play down my keenness.

Now look at the potential customer's tension for change.

Figure 14: Assessment of the gap – analysing tension for change

ASSESSMENT OF THE TENSION FOR CHANGE			
Supplier		**Customer**	
Ideal outcome: • Customer agrees to become a regular account • Opportunities to cross-sell our product range • Customer accepts this contract on our quoted terms and conditions	10	**Ideal outcome:** • Supplier alters their contract to meet our production schedule • Supplier accepts our request for special packaging • Supplier agrees to reduce their price by 5%	10
Current situation: • Customer has not bought from us in last five years • May not agree to our terms and conditions • Has potential to become a profitable account • Is a large buyer of our main product range, but sources it from our competitors!		**Current situation:** • We source from three companies, all similar • An extra supplier would be useful, but not needed at the moment • If they could meet our production schedule and reduce their price by 5% we would benefit	
Your rating of the current situation (1–10)	2	Your rating of the current situation (1–10)	6
Tension for change	8	**Tension for change**	4

Although they would be happy to transfer some of their purchasing dollars to this supplier, they have long-standing and good relationships with other suppliers. Price is important to them, and if a competitive deal in terms of price, delivery and servicing was offered, they would consider making a change. So their tension for change is quite low – a 4.

What does that mean? If you are the customer, you can be relaxed about whether you get a deal or not, though you are quite happy to try them out. After all, reducing costs of raw materials is always high on your agenda. And they do have a number of other products we could use. So a deal is certainly possible, providing the terms are advantageous to you. You also guess that they would like you as a customer, as they have been trying to secure some of your business for years. Maybe you can use that to your advantage!

For the supplier, that 4 is a problem. It means they really don't need you. However, they are willing to negotiate on this quote, so I will need to build up their tension for change by highlighting the benefits of dealing with us. There are a number of things they don't appreciate, like our computer system that allows them to order direct from our stores, and our technical service which is superior to anyone else's and free to major customers.

So you can see that assessing tension for change shapes the way you do your preparation and how you structure your proposals. It allows you to innovate where appropriate and exclude aspects which would be of high cost to you and of little value to them. Overall it provides a level of confidence in the approach you take.

A word of warning! Although you can assess your tension for change very accurately, your assessment of theirs is based to some extent on perception, or assumptions. If your market intelligence is reliable, your assessment will be close. If it is guesswork, then factor that in and make sure one of the first things you do on meeting is check out your assumptions. There's nothing more embarrassing than blowing it at the beginning of a negotiation!

What is your BATNA . . . escape to what?

Whatever your tension for change quotient, you need a BATNA. And the higher your tension, the more important having a BATNA becomes. So what is a BATNA?

The term BATNA was introduced by Roger Fisher and

William Ury in *Getting to Yes*, and it is now very much part of international negotiation language. Best Alternative To a Negotiated Agreement is what it stands for, and you need one!

One of the problems that faces all negotiators is what happens if we can't reach an agreement. No-deals are quite common, but if the consequences of a no-deal are that business does not happen, orders are cancelled, customers are not supplied, parts are not delivered, or servicing not done, then that is serious.

Sometimes it's simple. Using the example above, the potential customer has no real need of a BATNA as they will be in no worse a position if they don't get a deal. But for the supplier a BATNA could be agreement to quote again on the next tender, an opportunity to provide a sample supply, an agreement to demonstrate their direct ordering system, and so on.

Referring back to the guitar and amplifier situation, Bruce's BATNA may have been to ask for the special-offer price on the guitar and buy the amplifier he wanted separately; or buy the set, sell the lower specified amplifier through his contacts, and then buy the amplifier he required; or go to another dealer who had the required combination and negotiate with them, using the other dealer's special offer as a leverage.

The key point to having a BATNA is to think about it, and if necessary prepare for it, in advance. After all, it's no more than contingency planning!

Key Point Summary
- We conduct a gap analysis for each party – the difference between their current reality (where they are now) and their desired outcome (where they would like to be)
- We can assess the actual gap for ourselves, and a perception of their gap
- The gap creates a tension for change
- Tension for change is like a piece of elastic – the wider the gap, the stronger the tension
- When the tension for change is high for only one party, they are at a disadvantage and may give away variables in order to achieve their desired outcome

- When the tension for change is equal, a balanced negotiation is more likely
- Gaps can change as they are dependent on the current value systems
- A BATNA – a contingency plan and an alternative to a lose outcome, should be developed

▶ TRY IT OUT

In Figure 14 we have used a scale of 1 (low) to 10 (high) in assessing each party's tension for change. If they are 10, they're desperate! If they are 6 to 8, they are keen to do the deal. Less than 4 – it really doesn't matter to them whether they do the deal or not.

Here is a fairly typical family scenario at holiday time. How would you assess the tension for change, on the 1 to 10 scale, for the mother, the father, and the two teenagers? (Suggested ratings with reasons are included in the Appendix.)

Mother: Senior practice nurse in a large and busy community health centre. Last break was a week at home nine months ago. Looking forward to a three-week holiday in the sun at their friend's beach house, reading, swimming, walking and sleeping!

Father: Partner in a suburban accounting firm. Been overseas for two conferences this year, which included extra days sightseeing and relaxing. The senior partner has acquired a quarter share in an eight-berth cruiser, and has invited the family to join their family (two young children) on a two-week island cruise. Share the costs, and although a relatively expensive exercise, within budget. Would be great for networking at all the stopovers!

Teenagers: Missed the usual school holiday skiing week during the year as the parents couldn't arrange time off together, so were promised a special holiday – a week's skiing in Colorado was mentioned some months ago. Want something exciting, and definitely with lots of others their own age – so skiing would be great, but so would surfing!

7 | Variables – the ingredients of success

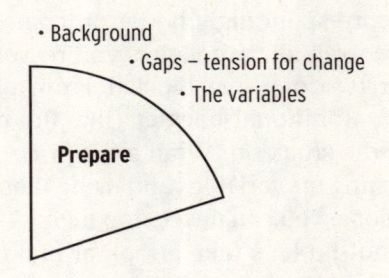

- Background
- Gaps – tension for change
- The variables

Prepare

▶Variables are to negotiation as ingredients are to cooking – essential. Negotiation relies on the ability of each party to trade, and the trading currency is variables. Items which are not tradable are often mistakenly labelled as variables, but should be termed items, issues or aspects. Like any trading game, the more variables at one's disposal the greater the opportunity to trade in one's own favour. Variables should therefore be broken down into the smallest manageable components. When considering the variables to incorporate into a negotiation we consider those that we must have (essentials) and those we would like to have (desirables). There will be some we are ambivalent about (non-essentials). Brainstorming and mind-mapping are two creative tools effectively used for sourcing and analysing variables.

The building blocks . . . better more than less

In the Introduction the term 'variable' was introduced, and we looked at some examples. Let's remind ourselves of what they are and why they are so important, in fact indispensable, to negotiation.

Remember the definitions of negotiation? The unique difference between a negotiation and any other transaction was that the parties had items of value, or variables, to trade. Without the ability to trade, there is no negotiation.

So variables are the building blocks for a good negotiator. Why more than less? Quite simply it is hard to build a decent structure with five or six Lego blocks. Most of us would like a box full – then we can really achieve something worthwhile! And it's exactly the same in a negotiation – the more variables you have at your disposal, the more creative and flexible you can be, with a correspondingly better outcome.

If you want to remain a haggler, you're very welcome to stick with your two or three blocks! From our experience, however, once a traditional haggler (like the old style buyer who got his needle stuck on 'What's the price?') gets into the practice of searching for variables and using them to good effect in their negotiations, you can never stop them! They get hooked – and so will you! So let's take a look at making the deck of variables bigger.

You're the local school treasurer and you have been getting quotes for the replacement swimming pool. The quote you like best is from a local contractor, Poolside, who specialise in pool construction and landscaping. Their slogan is: 'From go to stop, we do the lot.' However, it's not the cheapest. In fact it's several thousand over the budget approved by the school board. But you decide you'd prefer to negotiate a better deal with Poolside than work with the other out-of-area quotes. Having had some experience in financial negotiations, you know that having a number of variables to trade with always makes it easier. So you ask the school headmaster to join you in a brainstorming session. The list you came up with was quite extensive!

Looking at this list you see that there are some items which are fixed – that is they really can't be varied. And some come after the negotiation! So are these non-negotiables?

Non-negotiables . . . are they really?
The trouble with non-negotiables is their effect on our trading ability. So we need to decide which are truly fixed (and,

- Fencing – old, needs replacing
- Safety during construction
- Parent labour
- Price
- Budget approved
- Pupil labour
- Holidays or Term
- Removal of old pool
- Location of pool
- 'Poolside' advertising
- Dust
- Noise
- Extent of landscaping
- Removal of extra soil
- Progress payments
- Insurance
- Deposit
- Supervision
- Use during holidays
- Renting it out
- Existing pump
- Weekend working-bee
- Performance bond
- Council approval
- Painting existing sheds
- Planting trees
- Guarantees
- Servicing contract
- Pool cleaning
- Official opening
- Local business signs
- Local sponsorship

Figure 15: Brainstormed list of pool ideas – school

therefore, by definition not variables at all) and which could be varied if we were forced to. We need to sort them into non-negotiables and fixed, and indicate which of the non-negotiables are absolutely not able to be varied.

We'll come back to the two variables that we have labelled non-negotiables later, but for the moment let's look at those that are truly fixed.

Variables – the ingredients of success

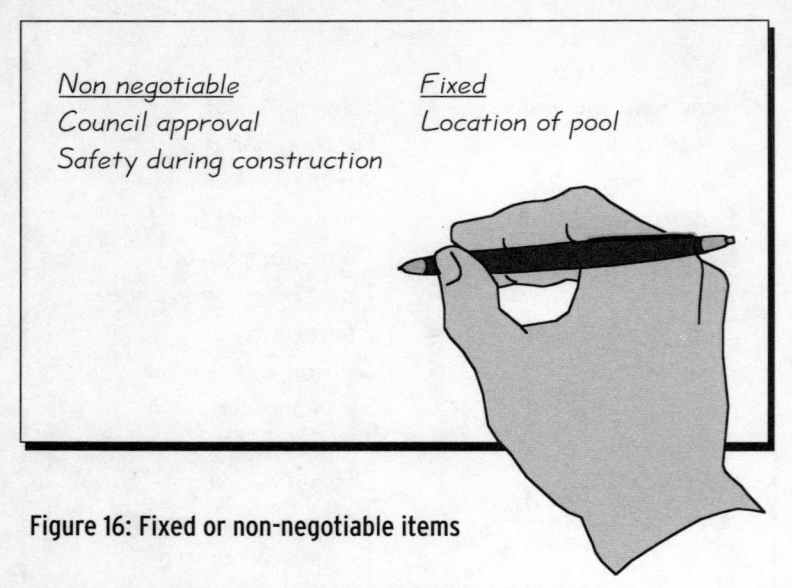

Non negotiable
Council approval
Safety during construction

Fixed
Location of pool

Figure 16: Fixed or non-negotiable items

The fixed aspects . . . don't forget their value
As we can see, we have listed only one! There are very few truly fixed aspects, and we must ensure we don't underestimate their importance. Just because the location of our house when we put it up for sale is fixed (you can't move it!) does not stop us from extolling the virtues of the location (close to schools, close to the reserve, ideal position for sun in winter, etc). So look for the benefits of the fixed aspects – what might be important to Poolside? The requirement that the new pool must be in the same position as the old can be a benefit: the old pool has to be removed, therefore a large hole already exists which will save digging and carting away; there will be no hidden obstacles under the earth as it's already a hole; the ground will be fully compacted so an engineer's involvement will be minimal; existing pump and drainage lines may be usable.

So when you have some fixed aspects, look for the positives, convert the negatives into positives, and actively 'sell' them during the negotiation.

The variables mind-map . . . clears the mind!
Brainstorming the list of variables in Figure 15 got everything out, but it is hard to group like items together from a list. This

is where mind-mapping comes into its own. And by doing one for our own situation, we stimulate our thinking about the other party's variables, and we can prepare one for them too. This helps us later when we assess the relative importance of each variable to each party.

If you want to try preparing your own mind-map from the list above, a blank mind-map format follows. A suggested completed one is shown in Figure 17 for you to compare. Figure 18 shows our perception of Poolside's situation. You will note there are many items that are common to both parties, though each have some that are important or relevant to their side only.

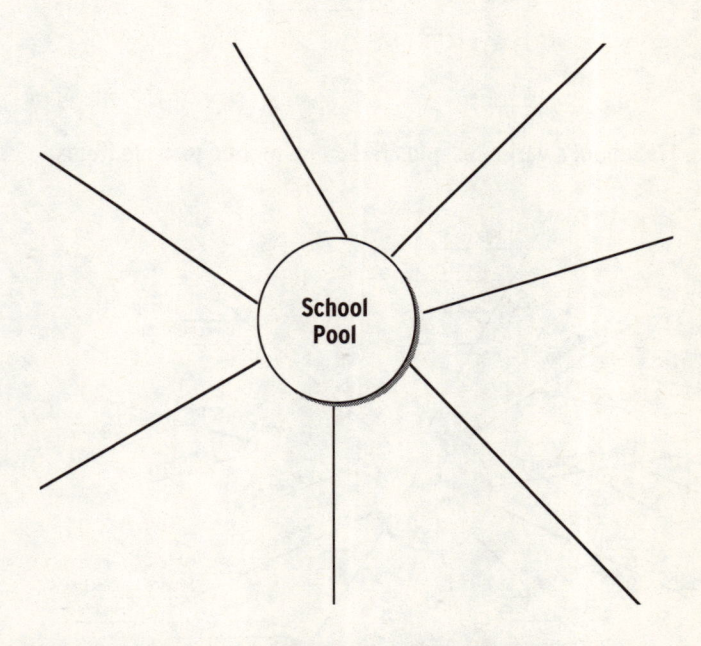

(Blank mind-map with central circle labelled "School Pool" and eight radiating lines)

Mind-map: School's variables and fixed items – you complete!

Some negotiation practitioners say you should only list the variables you have control over, but I find some overlapping does not matter at this stage, and it is better to include all aspects which will or may affect us or them. We can sort out the relevant control factors later.

Variables – the ingredients of success

Figure 17: School Pool mind map

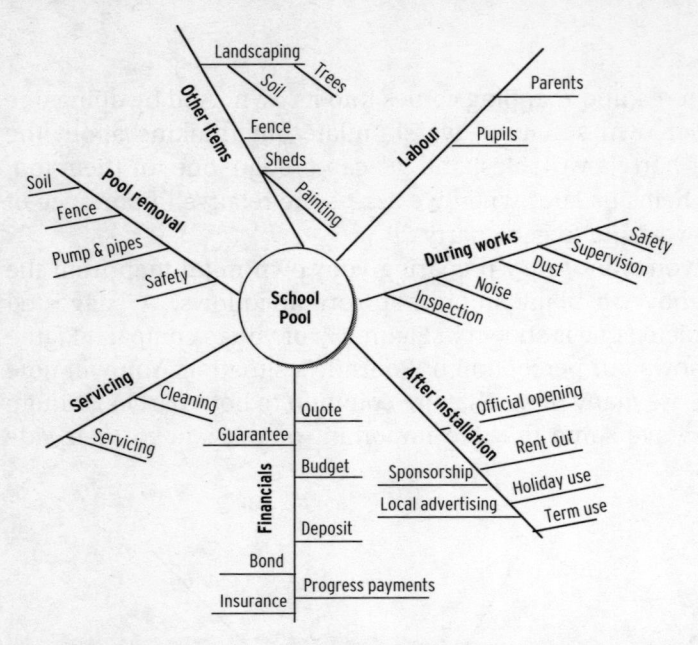

School Pool (center) with branches:

- **Other Items**: Landscaping, Trees, Soil, Fence, Sheds, Painting
- **Labour**: Parents, Pupils
- **During works**: Safety, Supervision, Dust, Noise, Inspection
- **After installation**: Official opening, Rent out, Holiday use, Term use, Sponsorship, Local advertising
- **Financials**: Quote, Guarantee, Budget, Deposit, Bond, Insurance, Progress payments
- **Servicing**: Cleaning, Servicing
- **Pool removal**: Soil, Fence, Pump & pipes, Safety

Figure 17: School's variables, plus fixed and non-negotiable items

Figure 18: School Pool – Poolside mind map

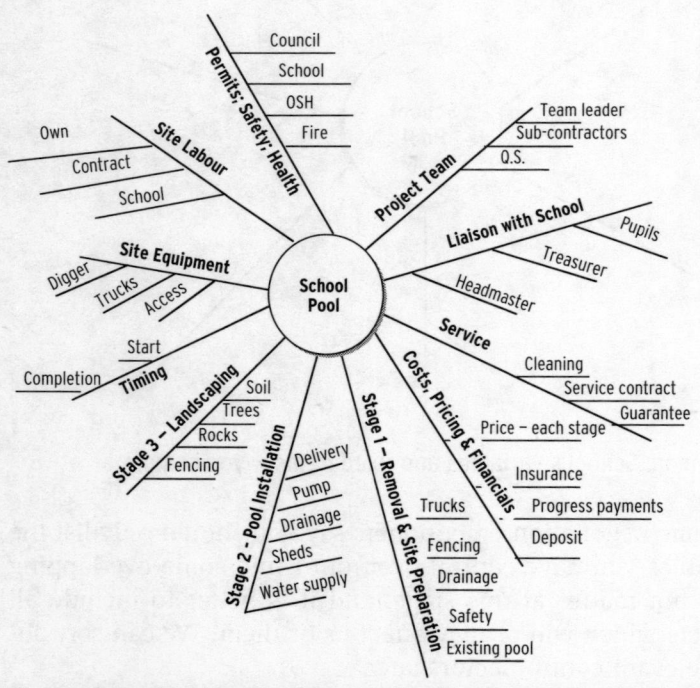

School Pool (center) with branches:

- **Permits; Safety; Health**: Council, School, OSH, Fire
- **Project Team**: Team leader, Sub-contractors, Q.S.
- **Liaison with School**: Pupils, Treasurer, Headmaster
- **Site Labour**: Own, Contract, School
- **Site Equipment**: Digger, Trucks, Access
- **Timing**: Start, Completion
- **Stage 3 – Landscaping**: Soil, Trees, Rocks, Fencing
- **Stage 2 – Pool Installation**: Delivery, Pump, Drainage, Sheds, Water supply
- **Stage 1 – Removal & Site Preparation**: Trucks, Fencing, Drainage, Safety, Existing pool
- **Costs, Pricing & Financials**: Price – each stage, Insurance, Progress payments, Deposit
- **Service**: Cleaning, Service contract, Guarantee

Figure 18: Poolside's variables, plus fixed and non-negotiable items

Negotiation Skills

Must-haves... and like-to-haves

Before we are in a position to rank the variables (ranking means looking at them from the viewpoints of cost and value, which we will do in the next chapter) we need to decide which aspects are very important to us, through to those we would be happy to give up. Sometimes this analysis is called the 'must-haves' and the 'like-to-haves'. That's pretty descriptive, and if you eventually find you prefer those two categories, that's fine. For more complex negotiations three categories are better.

- Essentials are those items that are integral to our position, and we will not agree to a deal if they are not included. (They are still tradable, but must be in the final settlement.)
- Desirables are those items which we would like to have included as part of the final deal. They would make the outcome more acceptable to us, however we would be prepared to leave them out if the overall package was satisfactory.
- Non-essentials are those items which we would be happy to leave out if required – they have little importance to us in the overall context of this negotiation.

Figure 19 sets out a possible scenario for the neighbours and the fence introduced in Chapter 3.

Priority	Neighbour – you	Neighbour – them
Essentials	New timber or new wire Finish by April 30 50/50 cost share	Cost – max $30 per metre 80% D.I.Y
Desirables	Timber D.I.Y. Removal by contractor Posts by contractor	New wire or timber Cost split 50/50 Start after January Finish by May Contractor < 20%
Non-essentials	Contractor Proportion wire: timber Cost Start date Fixing wire Fixing palings	Source of wire or timber

Figure 19: Relative priorities, fence

Figure 20 sets out a possible scenario for the school and Poolside.

Priority	For the school	For Poolside
Essentials	Safety Time of completion Supervision on site Performance bond Guarantee Council approval Pool location Pool price at quote	Deposit Contract Truck and digger access Pupil supervision Safety Time – of start – of completion Pool price > 90% quote
Desirables	New fencing Parent labour Pupil labour Painting existing sheds Time of start Service contract Use of existing pump Progress payments Dust control 5% pool price quote discount	Progress payments Use of school facilities Fencing contract Full landscaping contract Water supply Service contract Pool cleaning contract Pool price at quote
Non-essentials	Pool cleaning contract Noise control Tree planting Full landscaping contract	Parent labour Pupil labour Shed painting

Figure 20: Relative priorities, pool

In the You Try It section there's a mind-map and a variables analysis exercise for you to try your skills on.

Key Point Summary
- We need variables in order to trade
- The more variables we have, the more effective our trading is likely to be
- We initially prioritise the variables into essential, desirable, and non-essential
- We can use brainstorming and mind-mapping to prepare and prioritise the variables
- Some aspects are fixed; although we cannot trade them they are still valuable

▶ **YOU TRY IT**

Choose one of the following scenarios, mind-map and priority analyse the variables for the two parties. (Suggested mind-maps and priority analysis are included in the Appendix.)

1. You are moving to another location, and have decided to rent for a period while you look for a suitable home to buy. You and your partner both work, have two school-age children, and you want a three-bedroom place with reasonable grounds for outside play. You are meeting the owner of an advertised place which sounds suitable tomorrow.

2. You have been promoted to another division within your company, but are unhappy with the small increase in your package. You raised this with your new boss, who suggested you come and discuss it with them tomorrow.

8 | What's it worth?

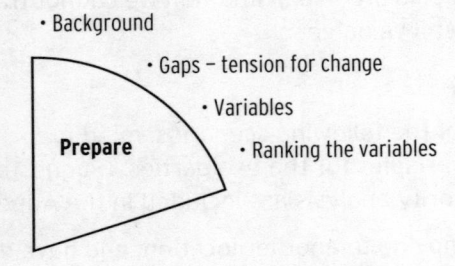

Prepare
- Background
- Gaps – tension for change
- Variables
- Ranking the variables

▶To be effective traders in negotiation, the relative costs and values of each variable must be known. The process of bargaining within negotiation is similar to most card games: aces are high value while fillers are the low numbers; major coloured cards are swapped or exchanged for similar worth, and a card that might cost the game is held on to. Bottom line depends on accurate assessment of trading values. Flexible thinking about relative values and perceptions is required as values constantly change.

The trading value of a variable ... what's it worth to them?

In the last chapter we sorted our variables into essentials, desirables, and non-essentials. We may prefer to call them must-haves and like-to-haves.

We did that to make sure that those aspects integral to an agreement were included, that any items not deal-breakers were recorded as desirable inclusions, and there were some that we were ambivalent about. We did this exercise for both parties.

We can now take those variables and rank them. Ranking means to sort them into four categories, based on their relative costs and values.

Why do we bother to rank them? Mainly to make sure that we get the best overall deal in terms of our bottom line. Even a simple situation such as negotiating with a family member over the use of the car in exchange for some extra help around the house is fraught with danger if you don't rank your variables before you start the seemingly innocuous negotiation. Your list, as the parent, includes washing, ironing, dishes, washing the dog, vacuuming bedroom, sweeping the path, pocket money, petrol payment, excess insurance bond, and curfew time on the weekends. Your oldest teenager is only concerned with having the use of your car as often and for as long as possible, and the money to run it! A teenager probably won't view it as a negotiation, but you must, otherwise you'll be – to use the colloquial term – screwed!

So what is of high value to them but won't cost you much? These are the best variables to trade – they give you high leverage. Let's say having their own say over how they spend your money is very important to them at the moment. You have to fork it out regardless – so it is of high value to them, but of relatively low cost to you. The time that they want the car for on the weekend is of high value to them, and of relatively low cost to you, as long as you have it to do the Saturday morning shopping. Again a high value to them, low cost to you.

You have just completed the process of ranking for those two variables. It wasn't that difficult, was it? Yet it is the single most important analysis you can do in any negotiation. The experts base whole negotiation preparations on ranking the variables.

The names given to these categories are self-explanatory, and you may be familiar with them as they are often used in public reporting of business or political negotiations: aces, trades or swaps, fillers, and no-no's. We'll consider each of these in turn, and then chart them out.

Aces
You've probably worked out that the two variables the mother categorised as having high value to the teenager, with a relatively low cost to her, were Aces. Correct! And the term is

apt. It is the best card in the deck; it is powerful, as in 'an ace up my sleeve'.

But it is only an ace for you if the other party is aware of its worth. So if the teenager thinks that the use of the car is a given and nothing is required of them in return, they will not place a high value on it. Similarly, if every time they have asked for money it has been given without restriction or limit, they will not place a high value on it. If they're made aware of the value, you can say: 'This is of value to you, so give me something valuable in return, like your time and co-operation!'

What might be an ace for the school pool contractor? Being able to start removal of the old pool the day after the school holidays commence, and having the new pool finished in time for the swimming sports three weeks later may well be of high value to the school and, provided the contractor manages their time and people resources well, of no extra cost to them. And having the children away improves the situation, as the dust and noise problem won't exist.

A word of caution about variables that are of low cost to you. You must view all your variables on the basis of value to the other party first. If you just consider the cost to you, you will find yourself donating variables that you should be using to best advantage for yourself. The rule is never donate, always trade. No matter how little it costs you, always put value on it, always get something in return. If you think about it, do you place value on things that are just donated to you? (Does 'here, it didn't cost me much so you may as well have it' sound valuable?) No. We tend to value more highly those things that have cost us something in return.

Swaps or trades

I prefer the term swaps as it conjures up a swap-meet where people exchange items of roughly equal worth. In terms of cost and value, swaps are just that: variables that are of high value to the other party and of high cost to you.

In business buy-sell negotiations, two common swaps are price and volume, but there are always exceptions. What might be a swap between the mother and teenager? Perhaps the curfew time could be extended by an hour in exchange for the

> Life consists not in holding good cards, but in playing those you do hold well.
> **Josh Billings**

paths being swept every Sunday. Both would be of relatively high value to each, and relatively high cost to both mother (worry) and teenager (precious time on weekend).

What about the school pool? A swap may be the school making a 50% deposit up front (high value to Poolside as they usually get payment on completion from school contracts; high cost to the school from loss of interest and possible leverage if things go wrong) in exchange for the contractor taking the demolished pool to the dump free of charge (money saved for the school therefore high value; high cost of truck and driver and disposal fees for the contractor).

You will usually find proportionately more swaps than any other ranking. They are the bread and butter of negotiation trading, mainly because good negotiators will have researched well, and come up with as many variables as possible to enhance the process and the eventual outcome.

Fillers

I will always remember a team of construction managers and engineers who came up with a list of 33 variables during a mind-mapping session, which quite excited them as before we started they thought they had only three: time, quality and cost. One of the engineers, who quite liked a beer at the end of each day, came up with the suggestion of a variable being a crate of beer ceremoniously lowered by crane onto the construction site every Friday night at knock-off time for the subcontractors and their teams. His suggestion caused quite a laugh, but I got them to think about what it was in terms of ranking. The choice was unanimous – a filler.

Now, fillers are colloquially called goodwill, give-aways, public relations, or ground bait (sprat to catch the mackerel). They regarded the crate of beer as goodwill and public relations, so we left it that way. A few weeks later we had another meeting and I asked them how the crate of beer on Fridays was going. They chuckled as they told me what had happened. 'We were all totally wrong about that one. The filler that we thought it was has turned out to be a flipping ace. It went down so well on that site, and had such a positive effect on relations between us and the subbies, that it's now company policy that all sites get the crate on a Friday night.'

Well, it would be nice to think that all your fillers could become aces, but that was a rare one! Nevertheless, fillers – low value to the other party and low cost to you – can be very useful. They can smooth something over and are often used to get over a hiccup on a minor issue; they can start things moving again; and they can make the other party feel you're thinking of them.

So what might be a filler for the mother? Perhaps paying her teenager the allowance weekly instead of monthly. Perhaps setting out the ironing board and sorting the clothes to be ironed. And for the school? Perhaps providing a key to the staffroom so that the contractors have easy access to hot water for their breaks. (I can see you turning that into an ace!)

No-no's

As the expression indicates, these are non-negotiables. You have considered these variables carefully and decided that because they are of no, or little, value to the other party, and are of high cost to you, it is not worth considering them for trading at all.

A common non-negotiable we all meet is documentation. Have you ever read your mortgage document? Or worse, your overdraft agreement? And for those of you in business, the debenture deed? Best not to! But if you ever try to draw lines through the clauses that offend you, no matter how plausible your argument, lenders insist that their document is sacrosanct. And you won't get your loan until it's signed and sealed. Now that's a non-negotiable. (I've often thought we should devise a similar document for borrowers which must be signed by the lender before a draw-down can be made! After all, they are moneylenders, the opposite of money-borrowers – but the agreements are a bit lopsided!)

Difficulties arise when you have too many no-no's. What you are in effect saying is 'these are fixed, non-tradable items'. That restricts you and may limit the outcome. So review any no-no's before you definitely rule them out of trading.

To make it pictorial, which helps us as we prepare for the negotiation, we have designed a form to use when ranking variables, and in Figure 21 we've used the school as the example. Consider the rankings we suggest – do you agree with them? You may have made different assumptions, and that will change the ranking and the way you would use that particular variable during the negotiation.

In the You Try It section at the end of this chapter, one of the exercises is to complete a ranking for Poolside, the contractors. Our suggested rankings are included in the answer section in the Appendix.

	Low Cost to School (Us)	High Cost to School (Us)
High Perceived Value to Poolside (Them)	**Aces** Flexibility of timing–start New fencing contract Full landscaping contract Service contract Pool price at quote	**Swaps or Trades** Timing – completion Pool cleaning contract Shed painting contract Progress payments Deposit amount Site supervision Parent labour Tree planting Pool price discount
Low Perceived Value to Poolside (Them)	**Fillers** Truck access Water supply Use of school facilities Use of existing pump Pupil labour	**No-no's** Performance bond Guarantee Site safety Council approval Pool location

Figure 21: Ranking the variables for the pool – school

What's it worth?

Your bottom line depends on it . . . so rank them with care!

Why have we stressed the importance of ranking the variables? Quite simply your bottom line depends on it. If you give away your aces, you lose your primary strengths. If you give away your swaps, or exchange them for lesser value in return, you will lose something every time. If you haven't thought carefully about your no-no's, you'll end up making a loss on each one.

Negotiation is about trading, so you have to make each trade count. It's the overall outcome, the total package, that you want to be a win/win. And whether it is a win/win will ultimately rest on the sum total of all the trades you have made.

What's important to them . . . right now?

Needs, wants, desires, urgencies, situations, circumstances, problems, opportunities and so on constantly change. So we cannot automatically assume that what was important to the other party three months ago has remained the same. The company changes direction; different requirements for quality apply. A new boss is appointed; stricter control of inventory is instigated. A child starts university; a new set of money problems emerges. A merger takes place; export opportunities are expanded. Change to our own circumstances and those of our trading partners is continuous, so our reassessment of the relative costs and values of the variables must also be continuous.

When I was working in the financial services sector, we funded several large property developers. There was one particularly successful developer who had never used us, and we were always disappointed that they arranged their large borrowings from our competitors. However, they approached us for a quote on several million dollars to buy a site in the CBD. As the security and other risk factors all checked out, we went to work on the deal. Now, we made a basic assumption that the interest rate was critical – they would obviously be shopping around for the best rate, so we shaved point after point off ours to ensure we would get the business this time. We were so caught up in making sure that our rate was sharp, we didn't really listen to their other requirements – that they needed a decision by next Thursday, and funds would be drawn down the following day. We just assumed that was their normal way of doing business. Neither did we pay much attention to their request for the loan to be for a year and transferable to another security 'if they should sell within that time'. We had made the assumption that the rate was everything, and that's what we would get this deal on.

The outcome of this deal was a salutary lesson to all of us involved at our end. It turned out that the property they were buying on Friday morning for $10 million had already been on-sold for $14 million with settlement Friday afternoon – a fact we did not know but could have found out if we had researched a little. The reason they had come to us had nothing to do with the rate – they had temporarily reached the house limit with their main funders, and we were an ideal replacement as we had no limit at that stage! The reason for the urgency was that no other lender could arrange the funds in time. Again, something we could have found out! So within 24 hours they made a $4 million profit and had our very cheap money for another 12 months! They would have happily paid us top interest rates if we had asked – all they were concerned about was getting the money from somewhere urgently. We all learned that our perception of what is important may not be theirs, and that a decent amount of research should always be done to check their current values. (As it turned out, they eventually became regular clients, and we made up the margin we had given away on the next two deals.)

In the next chapter we're going to look at how we set our settlement outcome objectives – what we want to have achieved at the end of the negotiation.

Key Point Summary
- Each variable has a cost
- Each variable has a value
- We assess each variable for value and cost
- The best trades for us are high value to them, low cost to us
- High value to them, low cost to us variables are Aces – don't give them away
- High value to them but high cost to us are trades or swaps – exchange them for equal worth .

- Low value to them, low cost to us are fillers – use as goodwill or ground bait
- Low value to them but high cost to us – treat as non-negotiable
- Values change as circumstances and situations change – treat nothing as a constant

▶ **YOU TRY IT**

❶ Prepare a ranking matrix for Poolside. Don't get caught by using Figure 21 rankings as the base – that was the school's ranking! Before you rank each variable, ask yourself: 'What is this worth to them?' Then ask: 'What is its cost to me?' Then allocate it. When you have completed the matrix you can review it alongside the school's – you will be able to identify areas where trading will be easy and very beneficial to both parties, and other areas where there is likely to be some hard bargaining! Compare your rankings with the suggested answer in the Appendix.

❷ Select one of the scenarios you mind-mapped in the previous chapter. Prepare a ranking matrix. Remember the rule – first ask 'What is this worth to them?' and then 'What is its cost to me?'

9 | What do we want to achieve?

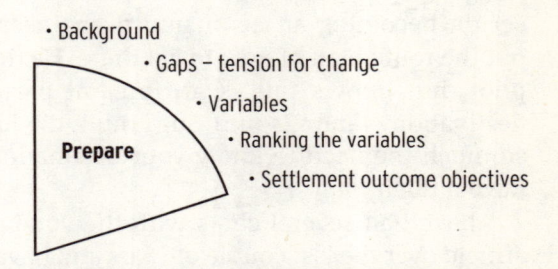

Prepare
- Background
- Gaps – tension for change
- Variables
- Ranking the variables
- Settlement outcome objectives

> At the fork in the road, Alice asked the Cheshire cat which road to take. The Cheshire cat asked, 'Where do you want to go?' To which Alice replied, 'I don't know.' 'Then,' said the cat, 'it doesn't much matter which way you go.' **Lewis Caroll,** *Alice in Wonderland*

▶When we enter a negotiation we must have planned and therefore prepared for a particular outcome. Although the outcome cannot be predicted in advance, it is strongly influenced by the expectations each party has, which in turn is based on their level of confidence in their preparation. There is sufficient research and anecdotal evidence that negotiators who aim high consistently achieve a higher level of outcome than those who think and plan passively. The simplest and surest method for managing the range and settlement points of a number of variables is to use a chart or map format. The final point of settlement is unknown until final agreement is reached, and the skills of the negotiator will largely determine the final outcome.

Without a flight plan . . . you're flying blind!
My younger son pays half the cost of his flying lessons, which means he values what he is taught. At 14 he sat his private

> The method of the enterprising is to plan with audacity, and execute with vigour; to sketch out a map of possibilities; and then to treat them as probabilities. **Bovee**

pilot's licence exams – our cost but his time and effort. He is set on becoming an aeronautical engineer and has mapped out the route plan of how to get there. He doesn't want to be a pilot, but knows this is an integral part of getting to his destination – and it's fun! But I think the lesson for me is not so much the need to know your destination, but the need to have a flight plan.

I have had several chats with the young instructors at the airfield over the last couple of years and have been consistently impressed with their polite, firm and no-nonsense attitude to contingency planning. For pilots, that's embodied in the flight plan, which charts their course to the destination and, in their case, the return. Even a short two-hour flight in the most beautiful weather requires one. It becomes a habit – on which their survival depends.

Now, we won't die, or cause the deaths of others, if we don't prepare our negotiation flight plan, but we will regularly get off course, and may sometimes completely miss our objective! This may only mean a lost friendship, an angry neighbour, a disappointed partner, an upset official – which are all bad enough. But in business it could cause a lost contract, a demotivated employee, a bottom line blow-out, a fall in share price, cancellation of an export order, or even bankruptcy. So flight plans are in!

In negotiation, flight plans are known as settlement outcome objectives.

- We must have somewhere to start – an opening or optimistic position.
- We must know a bail-out position – a final fall-back or pessimistic position.
- We must know the intermediate stops – realistic settlement positions within the range.

To know these, we need to know the relative costs and values of each variable. Much of this information will have already been prepared when we analysed and costed the variables, so it's more a matter of plotting the range and positions so you keep the whole package in mind during the negotiation.

Now, the range and points are not fixed from negotiation to

Variable	Priority*	Ranking†	Optimistic	Realistic	Pessimistic (bottom line)
Timing – start	DES	A	30 April	31 May	30 June
Timing – completion	ESS	S	31 July	31 Aug	30 Sept
New fencing	DES	A	$5000	$5500	$6500
Landscaping contract	NE	A	$8500	$10,000	$11,000
Service contract	DES	A	$500 pa	$550 pa	$600 pa
Pool cleaning contract	NE	S	$50 visit	$75 visit	$100 visit
Shed painting contract	DES	S	$1500	$1800	$2200
Progress payments	DES	S	10%, 25%, 65%	Even spread	50%, 35%, 15%
Parent labour	DES	S	Use 50%+	Use <10%	Refuse!
Guarantee	ESS	N	10 yrs	8 yrs	5 yrs
Deposit amount	–	S	Nil	10%	30%
Pool price	ESS/DES	A & S	10% discount	5% discount	At quote
Site supervision	ESS	S	By Poolside	Shared	By school
Performance bond	ESS	N	$10,000	$7500	$5000

* ESS = Essential; DES = Desirable; NE = Non-essential
† A = Ace; S = Swap/Trade; F= Filler; N= No-no

Figure 22: Pool–school's settlement outcome objectives (selection)

> - *I want cost split, 50/50; but might go 60/40.*
>
> - *I want mostly timber; prefer no wire if possible.*
>
> - *Cost $40–$60 a metre if timber, $20 if wire.*
>
> - *Prefer new timber but check cost.*
>
> - *Could use a contractor; could do some ourselves.*
>
> - *When should we start? Need to finish by April.*

Figure 23: Fence-settlement outcome objectives list (unclear)

negotiation, even with the same party. Situations and values do change, as we've already noted, so be thoughtful when you're in a repeat negotiation.

In Figure 22 we've reproduced the chart that our negotiation graduates use when they are plotting their settlement outcome objectives. We've used the school pool negotiation as the basis, and you'll be able to track how the variables have been taken from our initial mind-map (Figure 18), the essentials, desirables, non-essentials analysis (Figure 19), and the ranking analysis (Figure 21).

Although we have left many of the minor variables out for simplicity and easier reading, the relationships between the variables are clearly shown and make it easier for us to manage the discussions about the variables during the actual negotiation. Even for something as simple as the neighbours' fence it is always useful to write them down in this format. You decide whether you would be better off going into the fence negotiation with a list (Figure 23), or the settlement outcome objectives chart (Figure 24).

For the sake of a few minutes' thought and putting pen to paper, I know which I'd rather have! Could be worth a

Variable	Priority	Ranking	Optimistic	Realistic	Pessimistic (bottom line)
Cost split	ESS	A	Us 40/60 them	50/50	Us 75/25 them
Materials	ESS	S	All new timber	New timber and new wire	Quality used timber and new wire
Cost – new timber	NE	S	$40 per metre	$50 per metre	$60 per metre
Cost – new timber and wire	NE	S	$30 per metre	$35 per metre	$40 per metre
Cost – used timber and new wire	NE	S	$18 per metre	$22 per metre	$26 per metre
Removal	DES	S	By contractor and truck	Contractor and us and truck	All D.I.Y. and trailer
Posts	DES	–	By contractor	D.I.Y.	Contractor and us
Fixing palings	NE	–	D.I.Y.	D.I.Y.	Contractor and us
Fixing wire	NE	–	D.I.Y.	D.I.Y.	D.I.Y.
Start	NE	S	Jan 31	Feb 28	March 31
Finish	ESS	N	March 31	April 15	April 30

Figure 24: Fence-settlement objectives chart (structured)

relationship; could mean I got a paling fence and paid for half; could mean I have $1000 to spend on a holiday!

An international negotiator who consults for major Australasian companies in Asia uses a different charting system. He plots each variable vertically, whereas we do it horizontally. He uses the three positions within a range, but he prefers his format as it enables him to graphically plot the final agreement against the initial objectives. Figure 25 shows this in action. For those readers who are graphically inclined, you may prefer this format.

There are two other points we need to consider when setting our positions.

The actual destination is not known until the journey is

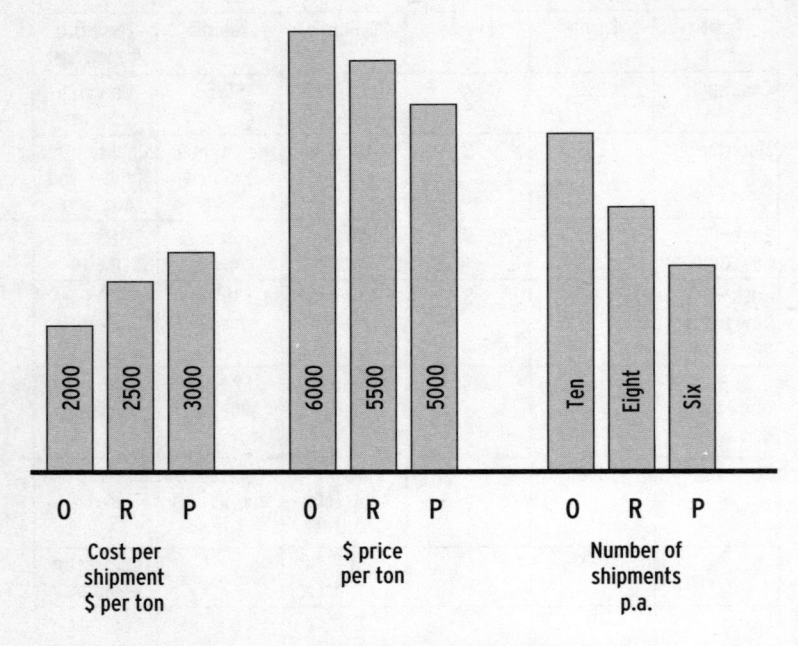

2000	2500	3000	6000	5500	5000	Ten	Eight	Six
O	R	P	O	R	P	O	R	P
Cost per shipment $ per ton			$ price per ton			Number of shipments p.a.		

Figure 25: Settlement outcome objectives—histogram format

completed. In many transactions, including problem-solving, the outcome can be closely predicted. In buy-sell transactions, the outcome is known in advance. But in negotiation, the final outcome is determined by the amount of preparation each party has put in, the ability to communicate effectively, the skills of trading, and the level of creativity contributed. Our students are amazed that we can give the same case-study briefs to several sets of negotiators, with the same rules and time frames, and the outcomes are totally different. It is also sobering to note that those who work for a win/win throughout the whole process almost invariably get the best overall deal.

There are dangers in setting our opening position too high or our bottom line position too low. If you have researched the other party, know your own situation and that of your competition, you should be able to calculate a range that will not offend the other party. That does not mean you shouldn't aim high – just not outrageously high. We are emotional beings – and our sense of 'fair and reasonable' is strong in negotiations.

I'm sure you can think of situations where you have felt personally affronted by an unreasonable request – and may even have refused to do business. We'll look at movement between positions when we consider trading.

Key Point Summary
- Negotiation objectives must be set in advance – settlement outcome objectives
- Value systems strongly influence objectives
- Objectives are set for each variable
- Settlement points are set within a range – optimistic, realistic, pessimistic
- Optimistic is the opening position – aim high
- Realistic is where you expect points of settlement will be
- Pessimistic is your bottom line for that variable
- A map or chart assists you control the trading of each variable
- A map or chart clearly shows relationships between variables
- Emotional outcomes must be taken into account

▶ **YOU TRY IT**

One of your work colleagues, a product manager, e-mailed a request for a meeting to discuss the resources they needed for a product launch. On the surface the request looks simple, but you, as sales manager, have a suspicion that if you are not careful about getting the real objectives out, you may end up having to meet most of the cost out of your budget, and worse, your staff might end up doing all the work! This must not happen!

Your colleague's request: 'I need two of your people to help with the customer survey, and run the focus groups. They'll enjoy it, and it will be excellent experience for them. Could Callum look after the analysis – he is a whizz with that computer! I'm of course looking after the agency – they seem to need a lot of hand-holding on this one. So could you get Kelly to organise the merchandising support for me – she knows them all so well it'll be a dream job for her. And with the sales teams, I'd really appreciate you briefing them on your

What do we want to achieve?

usual rounds. They'll take the launch in their stride if you just incorporate it into your usual pitch. Many thanks — I owe you on this one! See you Thursday to tidy up any other loose ends. Cheers!'

Prepare a mind-map of the variables, rank them, and set settlement outcome objectives. (A suggested answer is included in the Appendix.)

10 | Your shopping list – bringing it all together

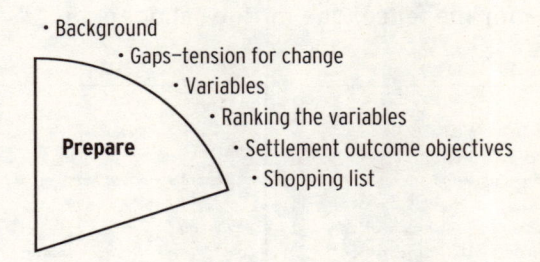

- Background
- Gaps–tension for change
- Variables
- Ranking the variables
- Settlement outcome objectives
- Shopping list

Prepare

▶ The preparation for a negotiation involves several steps. Each step expands and fine-tunes the previous step. The background summary leads into the gap analysis, which enables tension for change to be assessed. The brainstormed or mind-mapped variables are prioritised into essentials, desirables and non-essentials, and then ranked in terms of costs and values. Then a master chart of each variable, showing points of settlement within a range, is prepared – the settlement outcome objectives for the negotiation. Finally, a list of all the topics you want to include in the discussion is drawn up – aptly called the shopping list. This is prepared as a control document during the discussion stage to ensure only the items both parties wish to discuss are included in the negotiation.

You're going shopping . . . so make a list

Your shopping list is just that – a list of all the issues, items, aspects, etc, that you want to discuss. Some may be non-negotiables – you have to cover those. Some may not be variables but fixed aspects – you have to cover them. Think of the negotiation during this stage as a specialist store where you can find all the items you want, or at least ask for.

In point of fact, the list of variables you have on your settlement outcome objectives chart is the basis of your shopping list, but it doesn't have everything on it and is in a more complex format than you want as you work through the discussion stage with the other party.

So prepare a list just as you would for grocery shopping. You don't need to write 'matches, 2 boxes; quicklight, 10g'. 'Matches' is quite sufficient. Figure 26 shows two shopping lists – one for the fence, one for the school pool.

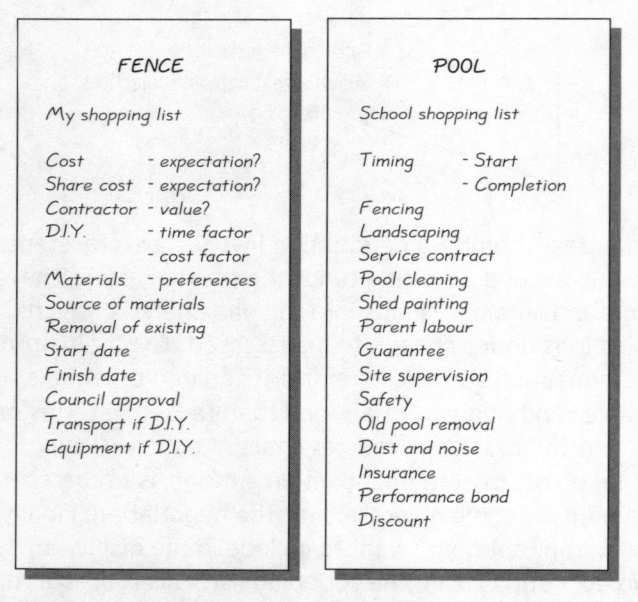

```
          FENCE                          POOL

My shopping list                School shopping list

Cost         - expectation?     Timing      - Start
Share cost   - expectation?                 - Completion
Contractor   - value?           Fencing
D.I.Y.       - time factor      Landscaping
             - cost factor      Service contract
Materials    - preferences      Pool cleaning
Source of materials             Shed painting
Removal of existing             Parent labour
Start date                      Guarantee
Finish date                     Site supervision
Council approval                Safety
Transport if D.I.Y.             Old pool removal
Equipment if D.I.Y.             Dust and noise
                                Insurance
                                Performance bond
                                Discount
```

Figure 26: Shopping lists (from settlement outcome objectives chart)

The consequences of not having a shopping list are quite high, as we find out when we are foolish enough to go to the supermarket without one. We end up with things we don't need (we may want them but that's not the point), important items like the fillings for the children's lunches are missed, and the check-out total is several dollars above the approved (family) limit. Negotiation is no different – if you go in without a shopping list you'll come away at the end with important aspects not covered, extra items that should have been avoided and, worse, the bottom line breached. Your partner, colleagues or boss have every right to question your negotiation ability.

At this point we are going to leave further consideration of the shopping list until the end of Chapter 14. We are effectively at the end of our preparation stage and are ready to meet the other party and start the face-to-face stages of discussion, expansion, trading and finalising.

Let's do a quick recap of our preparation.

First, we looked at the background to the negotiation – what we were negotiating, the people involved, and likely behaviours.

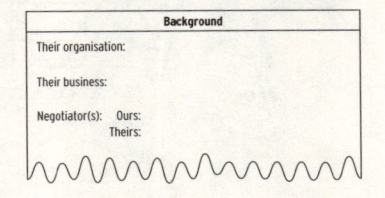

Figure 27: Background

Second, we assessed the tension for change – the gap between each party's current situation and where they would like to be.

Figure 28: Tension for change analysis

Your shopping list – bringing it all together

Third, we brainstormed or mind-mapped the variables that each party would need to cover.

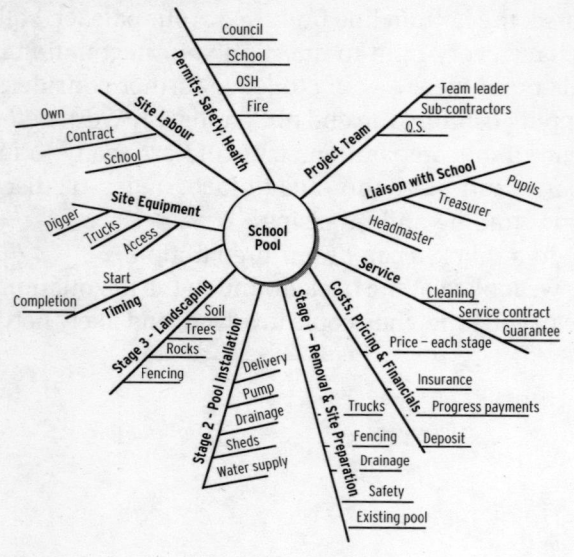

Figure 29: Variables—initial brainstorm (includes fixed and non-negotiable)

Fourth, we assessed the variables for each party into must-haves and like-to-haves, prioritising them into essentials, desirables and non-essentials.

VARIABLES: PRIORITIES		
Priority	For us	For them
Essentials		
Desirables		
Non-essentials		

Figure 30: Essentials, desirables, non-essentials

Fifth, we ranked the variables in terms of the costs and values – aces, swaps, fillers and no-no's.

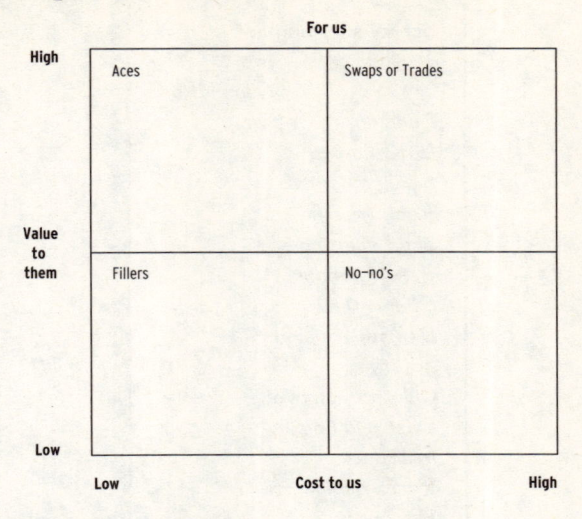

	For us	
High Value to them **Low**	Aces	Swaps or Trades
	Fillers	No-no's
	Low Cost to us **High**	

Figure 31: Ranking the variables

Sixth, we worked out the settlement ranges for each variable, deciding on optimistic (opening), realistic, and pessimistic (bottom line) positions.

Settlement Outcome Objectives

Variable	Priority	Value	Optimistic	Realistic	Pessimistic (bottom line)

Figure 32: Settlement outcome objectives

Seventh, we made a simple shopping list of the items needed to be covered during the negotiation.

```
            POOL
   School shopping list
   Timing      - Start
               - Completion
   Fencing
   Landscaping
   Service contract
   Pool cleaning
   Shed painting
   Parent labour
   Guarantee
   Site supervision
   Safety
   Old pool removal
   Dust and noise
   Insurance
   Performance bond
   Discount
```

Figure 33: Shopping list

We are now well prepared and ready to start the discussion!

Key Point Summary
- Preparing for a negotiation is essential
- Preparation involves research and reflection on facts and feelings
- The preparation stage involves several sequential steps:
  1. background (why we are there)
  2. gap analysis (where we are versus where we would like to be) for both parties
  3. the variables (the items, issues, aspects, etc, to be negotiated)
  4. prioritise the variables (essentials, desirables, non-essentials)
  5. rank the variables (aces, swaps or trades, fillers, no-no's) for both parties

6　settlement outcome objectives (optimistic, realistic, pessimistic)
　7　shopping list (items needed to be included in the discussion)
- There is no set time for preparation – whatever time it takes to do it thoroughly
- Good negotiators always ask 'what if' during their preparation
- Good negotiators ask for advice and information to verify their preparation
- Good negotiators think about and prepare for the discussion stage (meeting, location, timing, opening remarks, gaining win/win commitment, agenda)

▶TRY IT OUT

Score yourself on the checklist on page 104 – how well do you prepare for your important negotiations? (Some comments on your scoring are included in the Appendix.)

	Almost always	Often	Some-times	Seldom	Almost never
1. I write items down as I think of them					
2. I use some creative or lateral thinking tool to provide all the items I want to discuss					
3. I get someone to check my preparation					
4. I prepare a full shopping list before we start discussing					
5. I work out my must-haves and like-to-haves during my preparation					
6. I think about the negotiation from the other party's point of view					
7. I take the possible feelings about the negotiation into account during my preparation					
8. I have a bottom-line position for every item to be negotiated					
9. I start proposing from my optimistic positions					
10. I base my bargaining on the value of the variable to them and the cost to me					
11. I use fillers to get over minor stoppages (impasses)					
12. I work towards a win/win outcome					
13. I consider the other party's style of negotiating and adjust mine accordingly					
14. I prepare my opening (statement, gambit) to give me an initiative at the beginning					
15. I ask myself 'what if...' throughout my preparation					
16. I work out the gap between what I want and what I have					
17. I prepare a BATNA					
18. I sell the benefits of my 'fixed' items					
19. I break my variables into the smallest manageable chunks					
20. I prepare thoroughly for even minor negotiations					
Total ✓	×5	×4	×3	×2	×1
Total/100					

11 | Opening – initiate, gain, maintain

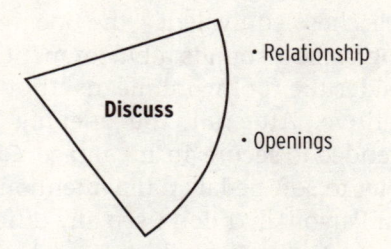

- Relationship
- **Discuss**
- Openings

▶ Captains like to win the toss as it gives them the initiative. They choose the opening move to secure the high ground. In negotiation the party who takes the initiative and gains the high ground may be able to maintain the initiative for some time, and may achieve a more favourable outcome. These early moves or opening gambits can be used with a win/lose or a win/win objective. The effect of an opening gambit is considered carefully and prepared in advance. Competitive openings can be effectively countered if they are recognised and their effect is known.

Who gets the toss? . . . it's your choice

When you get to call the toss at the beginning of a sports game, you like to win – it gives you the right to make the first decision. Which end you play from, whether you take the wind at your back at the beginning or the end, whether you have the sun behind you now or later, or simply start the game with the ball in your control.

In negotiation, it's also useful to get the toss – but the beauty is you get to decide whether you take the toss or not. It's your choice!

If you're familiar with the game of chess, you'll know that

white has the first move. It is the favoured colour, as the first move in chess tends to dictate the next few moves, and the initiative is often held by white for some time. (I always insisted playing white with my elder son because I could make the game last a few moves longer. If he got white I was almost certainly doomed to be checkmated within ten moves – and he was only eight years old!)

The relevance of the chess analogy is that the opening of a negotiation is very important – it's like choosing your weapon in a duel. And so the first moves in a negotiation have been called after their chess equivalent – the opening gambit.

Now, opening gambit sounds a bit competitive – especially when you consider the root word means 'tripping up'! And it can be competitive. After all, the opening manoeuvre or comment is intended to secure an advantage. Given that, some negotiators prefer to soft-pedal on the intention, and call them opening tactics. Personally I don't see any difference – tactics sounds just as intentional as gambits. Use whichever term you feel more comfortable with.

They are nevertheless extremely important to the negotiator, in any type of negotiation. Research indicates that in negotiation, as in chess, if the opening gambit is used appropriately, the initiative will be maintained and may well affect the final outcome. It also has a direct effect on the tone of the discussion at the beginning, and this also may influence the final outcome. Therefore, we suggest that you think very carefully about the early stages of discussion, and spend time working on your opening gambit.

Proactive . . . not reactive and defensive

It takes a little thought, but the difference between a prepared opening gambit and an obviously lazy approach is immense. Which of these pairs of opening gambits do you think would be more effective:

'Guess we'd better discuss the allowance you want.'

'I know you have asked for an increase in your allowance, Nicky, but there will have to be some changes to the weekend routines if I'm to consider it.'

'Do your results so far really warrant the normal level of bonus?'

'I am willing to discuss a bonus, but the results achieved so far could not justify the level we've paid in the past.'

'The quote you've given us looks pretty good, but we wonder whether you'd consider increasing the number of deliveries if you have the trucks available.'

'Thank you for your quotation. We've looked at it carefully, and in most areas it meets our requirements. However, there are specific aspects, one of which is delivery, that my company would like me to explore with you to see if we can better meet our changing distribution requirements. I suggest we isolate the issues where further discussion is needed and concentrate on those.'

The difference is obvious! To assist you to prepare, here are some of the more common opening gambits which you can adapt for any negotiation situation.

Opening gambits

1. Adjusting their expectations
Use when you wish to make the other party rethink and adjust their settlement objectives.

Parent to teenager negotiating home time after parties: *'Talking to other parents, it seems that 11 to 12 o'clock is the typical curfew time. So I'm prepared to look at midnight, provided I'm happy with the designated driver arrangement.'*

Prospective tenant to landlord negotiating a house rental: *'The rents around here are about $200, but they're for three bedrooms, whereas yours is only two. So I expect you'll be wanting $140.'*

2. Need to settle
Use to find out, or build up, their urgency to achieve a settlement.

National retailer to supplier negotiating new product supply: *'I understand you're wanting to launch before Christmas to establish your brand during the peak selling period!'*

Supplier to retailer negotiating delivery of next shipment:

'The exchange rate has been down for three weeks, and our next shipment is likely to cost 15% more.'

3. Neutralise strengths and weaknesses
Use when you want to downplay their strength(s).

Employer to applicant with highly sought-after specialised skills negotiating employment contract: *'Normally we're hard put to find someone with your qualifications, but the government's recent change on immigration has opened it up.'*

Use when you want to minimise your weakness.

Homeowner negotiating the 'redo' of their poor attempt at a do-it-yourself renovation with a builder: *'We're quite happy to live with it, but if we ever decided to sell we'd probably need to get it fixed.'*

4. Reveal another party
Use to show the other party they are not the only option.

House-seller to prospective buyer negotiating a conditional agreement: *'Although I'm prepared to consider a conditional offer, I do have another family from out of town who have sold up and can go cash unconditional immediately. They're coming with their lawyer tomorrow.'*

5. Set up a straw man
Use to create a strong impression of a minor point as a must-have requirement which can be used when trading.

Homeowner negotiating landscaping contract with landscaper: *'One thing I must make clear right from the start. The job must be completed, at the very latest, by 30 November.'*

6. Adjust the power balance
Use to increase your power gradient.

Brother introduces elder sister into his negotiation with parents: *'Ann had this same situation last year, and she has points to make which should help us all think objectively about it'*

Young employee brings an older relative/acquaintance to a negotiation involving a complex employment contract: *'I've brought my aunt along. She's the financial controller for International Corp.'*

Supplier takes their lawyer to negotiation involving an

overseas contract: *'Hello, Margaret. I'd like to introduce Kevin, our company lawyer. He's an expert on international transactions, so he'll be able to help us through the grey areas.'*

7. Complain about past mistakes
Use to put the other party on the back foot.

Customer to supplier, negotiating new supply: *'Before we start, I'd have to say I was disappointed with the level of service I got when I needed supplies in a hurry last month. It took 48 hours, and I lost a full day of production.'*

A final word. Opening gambits can focus on any outcome. Traditionally they have been viewed as a tactic to achieve a win/lose. As you can see from the examples above, each one is equally available to be used to set up and encourage a win/win – and that is the way we would suggest most of your negotiations should be shaped.

The examples also indicate how to manage, or counter, the other party's opening gambit – look for the intent and respond positively.

'Your proposed scheduling seems OK, but your cost structure for the variations is totally over the top. My financial controller nearly had a heart attack. Come on you guys – get real!'

This could be met with: *'We're very real. It was your controller who insisted we make the changes, and we warned him at the time that the rescheduling would be an expensive exercise. Our accountant has checked the revised estimates, and our margin has not changed. And that margin was initially agreed to cover the total contract, including any variations. Perhaps we should be focusing on the variations, rather than the costs.'*

Of course, if you wanted to be snowed, you could have reacted with *'Oh, are they? I guess we'd better go over them again to see if we can get them down. What does your controller think they should be?'*

To sum up your opening gambit . . .

Don't wing it – plan it, prepare it, practise it, present it!

Key Point Summary
- Well considered and prepared openings can gain the initiative
- It is difficult to regain a lost initiative
- Initiative in the early stages can be gained through using an opening gambit
- Opening gambits are specifically designed to gain initiative
- Opening gambits can be used positively for a win/win, or negatively for a win/lose
- Opening gambits can support preconditioning activities
- A knowledge of opening gambits is essential to counter negative or competitive openings
- Good negotiators plan and practise their openings
- Good negotiators use opening gambits to control a win/win process

▶ YOU TRY IT

Categorise the following opening gambits as Aggressive, Assertive or Passive, and Win/lose, Win/win or Lose/win intent. (Answers are included in the Appendix.)

1. 'The last box you sent me was badly damaged. I can't afford the time to get replacements. We must arrange a more secure delivery.'

2. 'That last box you sent was a write-off! The time it took to get replacements was ridiculous. You'll have to get it right this time or you can forget it!'

3. 'It was a pity that the last box you sent arrived damaged though your people did do a good job getting me replacements. Can we see if we can improve the delivery this time?'

4. 'You surely can't be serious! You expect me to recommend that proposal to the committee with your track record? I'd want the biggest guarantee you've ever arranged to even consider signing it off.'

5. 'I couldn't consider signing it off unless you were prepared to arrange a significant guarantee. Your track record

doesn't engender confidence, though I know you will deliver perfectly on this one.'

6. 'I wish I could give you the week's extension Karen, but the other couple are willing to sign up tomorrow.'

7. 'It's a bit disappointing that the Council has changed the rules since we applied. I didn't think that would have affected us.'

8. 'Rules can be changed, but I object to them being retrospective. How do we get this through on the basis that we applied five months before the rule was changed?'

9. 'If we can't get this contract sorted out today, I'll have no option but to involve my financial controller. She is becoming very frustrated with the delay.'

10. 'The time this is taking is driving my financial controller up the wall. She's liable to cancel the whole contract if we don't finalise this before five. So let's move it!'

12 | Preconditioning – thinking way ahead

▶Setting someone or something up may be considered manipulative. In negotiation it is a legitimate strategy to exert control or influence the process or outcome. To be fully effective preconditioning needs to be planned and instigated early in the preparation stage, and reinforced throughout the whole negotiation.

If you want the outcome you want . . . then plan for it!
Preconditioning – another common word that negotiation has adopted as part of its terminology. The word 'conditioning' does have some negative overtones from a psychological point of view – altering the response of a person to a particular stimulus or situation. And with the 'pre' added it seems more manipulative – presenting the situation so that one stimulus automatically evokes another.

For example, 'poor service' and 'contract cancelled' are two situations that could be presented successively without reinforcement to become associated, so that when one is mentioned the other is immediately associated with it. If I am a supplier and my customer says anything about 'poor service' I will immediately think 'contract cancelled' – and probably work very quickly on getting the service right!

If we think about the preconditioning that we have done all our lives with family, friends and colleagues, there is not too much to be concerned about if we also use it in negotiation.

The key for negotiators is thinking way ahead. In most cases it means thinking before starting the preparation, and planning the preconditioning throughout the preparation and discussion stages. You have to put yourself in the other party's shoes before the negotiation situation is even contemplated, and then think forward to the end result you want them to achieve. Say you want your business partner to take over one of your existing clients. If you simply ask them to, they are likely to refuse. So you need to precondition them to the change. You could begin the process by casually mentioning the steady growth that has occurred with that client and that at some stage they may require more specialist advice than you can provide. You might indicate that they are looking for fresh ideas from others. You might add that they could well be the entrée to the new target market your partner has been wanting to break into. These suggestions could spread over days, weeks or even months. When the time is appropriate to negotiate on a change, they will be more conditioned to the idea and raise less resistance. They may become so accustomed to the idea that they initiate the change for you!

On the basis that actions by you are required, what avenues are available to you?

Telephone: The phone is a convenient and non-threatening medium to use when setting up a flow of suggestions leading to conditioning. It's quite possibly the salesperson's – and the politician's – best tool.

Letters: A more formal method than the phone, but you're more able to control the words actually used. Although a letter will be written with the recipient in mind, it is open to interpretation and an incorrect message may be received.

Articles: Always the favourite for someone who wants to get their point across without specifically pointing the finger. In negotiation situations, articles are often written for use after publication, which adds weight in terms of credibility. The initiator's viewpoint is designed to invoke support from the recipient, so they are more favourably preconditioned when a proposition is made or a meeting requested.

Third parties: Relationships are ultimately based on interactions between people. People prefer to deal with those

> **Failure to prepare is preparing to fail.**
> **John Wooden**

whom they trust and like. So preconditioning through others is the most actively used method. Think about these events:

'Her company has an excellent reputation, and she's the local expert in your technology. If she does contact you, I'd definitely take the opportunity to meet her.'

'I know Ralph has been on at you about re-negotiating that service contract with Staykleen, and I also know you would prefer to get some quotes. But I heard the other day from one of my bigger clients that Staykleen are installing the latest digital printing technology, and their current clients get first options on using it. And in the first year they're keeping their charges the same as now.'

You can appreciate the powerful effects of these third-party suggestions, all initiated by the negotiator who wishes to start the other party thinking!

In summary, preconditioning is not manipulation – which is the negative connotation. Used in the positive sense, it is managing the outcome and done with a win/win intention. Managing the negotiation from start to finish is the responsibility of the negotiator, which includes preconditioning when required to achieve the outcome.

Key Point Summary

- Managing the outcome is a legitimate and responsible activity
- Setting up a stimulus to influence an action to support the outcome may be required
- Preconditioning is a common strategy used in most negotiations, intentionally or unintentionally
- When used intentionally it can influence positively or negatively
- An understanding of preconditioning enables recognition and counter measure if necessary

- Preconditioning is a planned and usually prolonged activity

▶ YOU TRY IT

This is a reflective personal exercise. Thinking ahead through the next two to three weeks, envisage a simple negotiation situation at home or work. Run the situation through your mind, concentrating on the likely interchange of conversation. When you come to a point that causes the other party to back off – stop. Write the point down. Over the next few days think about that point and how you might influence the person or the situation so that the problem point is minimised. Then design a preconditioning strategy to achieve this.

An enlightening experience is to listen to a news item about a current controversial topic where pro and con proponents are being interviewed. The preconditioning will leap out! Try it!

13 | Control the process – manage the outcome

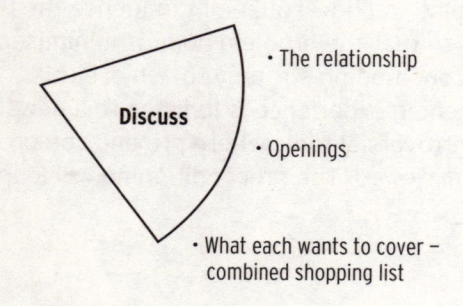

Discuss
- The relationship
- Openings
- What each wants to cover – combined shopping list

▶ The skilled negotiator understands that the process drives the outcome. There is a well proven structure and logical order which ensures that the negotiation stays on track. Best win/win outcomes are achieved when the process is followed. There are several steps within the discussion stage. Following introductions, and establishing or confirming rapport and relationships, the joint commitment to a win/win is sought. If outcomes are contrary, then the parties may need to reassess their approach. The broad objectives of the negotiation are then agreed. Opening gambits may be used at any time during the discussion stage. When these preliminary steps have been completed, it is possible and useful to agree an agenda. The detailed steps of obtaining and agreeing a combined shopping list concludes the discussion stage.

The process drives the outcome . . . be the driver

Process can be boring, but when the outcome is reliant on a process being followed, who has the luxury of being bored?

And the thing that excites the business people we train in negotiation skills is that they become the driver!

I was reading one of our graduate's feedback notes the other night, and I noted down a few of her comments about her ability to drive the negotiations through managing the process:

'I now focus on my own strengths and use my own power constructively to drive the negotiation. I always ask myself: "What do I want to get out of this negotiation?" and this drives my preparation. I'm more aware of how productive it is to maintain a forward momentum during the negotiation and maintain steady control. I'm constantly keeping a good record of progress during the negotiations and more than often I find myself going back over these notes . . . enforcing a positive result which I have seen build the relationship, making it stronger and last longer.'

So let's follow the process round the discussion stage.

Direct the show . . . set the scene

It is always preferable for the negotiation meeting to take place under your control. So if there is a choice, choose your place. For the teenager negotiating with father, don't try and conduct the meeting in the father's territory – try and find a neutral place, like the dining-room. (His study holds power for him, not you.) If as mother you're negotiating with your teenager, don't do it in their bedroom – they're more likely to lie on their bed and argue! Get them into your territory.

If it's the neighbours, get them into your place or your garden – you can control the process far easier in your domain.

If it's the boss you're negotiating with, they'll probably insist that it be in their office or area (remember they've probably been on a negotiation seminar!). However, try for a neutral place such as an interview room. And make sure you have organised privacy and coffee if you want it to be a long meeting.

For business meetings, internal or external, always try for your place. The general rule is 'selling at their place, negotiation at ours'. You find out all you want to know when you visit them, but conduct the negotiations in a situation under your control.

First impressions . . . they really count

If you know the other party, then formal introductions are out. But even with acquaintances, or neighbours or professional colleagues, the way you 'meet and greet' conveys an impression that may well influence their attitude towards you and therefore the negotiation itself.

With parties you have not met, start the introductions in a manner that is appropriate to the type of negotiations they are. This will usually mean slightly more formal than you would usually conduct ordinary meetings, but still friendly and professional. If they are team negotiations, then check the hierarchy before they arrive and ensure you know their names, positions and who the lead negotiator is.

Remember that first impressions, gained in the first 10 seconds, can last a long, long time!

Look after their feelings . . . we're all emotional beings!

Build rapport – we must have heard those two words a thousand times. And you'll probably hear them another thousand! Ask yourself: 'How would I like to feel in their position?' and then convert that to: 'How do I want them to feel right now?' Then act on that.

It's not so much the words that you use to put them at ease, or whatever feeling you want them to have, but the way you say the words and the way you conduct yourself. It's the non-verbals that count the most, especially when their senses are heightened, which is almost inevitable in a negotiation situation. We are emotional beings, so look after the feelings.

One of our senior associates was talking with me about industrial negotiations he had been involved with a few years ago. These were tough and competitive, with bullying, threats and intimidation. Walk-outs were common practice. Personalities and entrenched positions dominated. They took four to five days to reach an agreement, and both sides argued vehemently about everything. He said that one day the lead negotiator from the other party was ill, and they had replaced him with another member of their team. When they walked into the negotiation room on the first morning, there were pots of tea and coffee on the table, and muffins and cookies on plates. And the new lead negotiator was smiling, and welcomed them, and conducted the introductions! Now this could have been a tactic (an opening gambit) to soften them up and then hit them, but it wasn't. The negotiations proceeded through the steps of a well-conducted negotiation, and although they had their differences on several issues, they were argued on the basis of the issues and problems, not the personalities and positions. The negotiations were completed in two days, and the outcome was the best win/win that either party could remember.

So how are your interpersonal skills looking?

Reinforce your preconditioning . . . and present your opening
We covered preconditioning in the last chapter. You should be looking for opportunities to reinforce the messages sent earlier. It may be a simple repeat: 'I'm glad you had a chance to read that report, Jim. It made very interesting reading, considering that's where this product ends up.'

Or it may be more subtle: 'We've given quite a lot of thought to what we discussed during our phone conversation last month, and we're not unhappy with your line of thinking.'

'What about my opening gambit?' I can hear you asking. Yes! Although you may have already stated it. For example:

If you are negotiating an increased loan with your banker, and you think they're going to really insist on personal guarantees, you may well have greeted your banker, not with a smile, but: 'Do you know what Credit Bank did to my production manager last week? They had the damned cheek to ask him for a personal guarantee on a loan. Hell, he's got no more borrowed than I'll have! With the same net worth! We both told them where to go, and he arranged it without any silly guarantees through First Bank – no hassles! Come on in. Sit down. Would you like tea or coffee?'

However, it is more common in win/win negotiation settings to employ the opening gambit after the introductions have been completed and you are sitting down. But do take the initiative wherever possible, and use the suggested tactics outlined in the previous chapter.

Be alert for power plays . . . make the power gradient work for you

The subject of power is very important in negotiations, and Chapter 18 is devoted exclusively to power and the power gradient. So at this point of the process, early in the discussion stage, we will make statements only. After you have read Chapter 18, you can refer back to this point.

Be alert for overt use of position power; they may try to intimidate you. Counter with high personal power. That will earn their respect during the discussion stage, and should have evened the power gradient by the time the shopping lists are confirmed.

Welcome decision power, as it may make the expansion stage more creative and will certainly enhance trading.

Welcome personal power, and learn from it. However, don't be overawed just because they appear to be an expert, or have a string of letters after their name. Real personal power in the other party will enhance a negotiation if you learn to harness it. Balance it by using all your power sources.

Set the agenda . . . control the time

If you get frustrated at meetings that go nowhere, you'll know that negotiations without an agenda drive you spare. But wait – there can be dire consequences when we have the attitude: 'Oh for goodness' sake, let's get these final matters discussed and out of the way, sign it off, and go home. We've covered most of the items.' No! No!

Research on major business negotiations shows that 80% of the trading value is done in the last 20% of the negotiation time. That means that the items you may have come to tentative agreements on are small in monetary terms, but large in operational terms. If you rush the trading because you have run over time, you could well sacrifice significant bottom line. And no one is justified in doing that – whether it's personal or business.

So an agenda is required. It is largely a process agenda, though time and people will be factors. If it's a business negotiation, say something along these lines:

'I suggest we start by confirming that our objective for this meeting is to reach an agreement on this contract that we are both comfortable with. To do that we will need to reiterate the issues and items that each side needs to have covered in detail, and then to look at areas where we agree, and those where differences exist. We can explore the differences, looking for options and alternatives that may suit us both. After that there may be some items that need trading off. We can then write up the total deal and pass it to our respective legal people for the final documentation. Is everyone happy to proceed on that basis?'

If it's a personal negotiation, say something along these lines:

'I'm sure you don't want to spend the rest of the day deciding how we're going to do this, so I've got my list ready, and I'm sure you've got your list too. So I suggest we chat those through. Those that we can't agree on we'll toss around and see if we can find a solution that suits us both. If there's anything left at the end, then both of us may have to compromise on something. OK with you?'

Most people in a negotiation appreciate having an agenda and, as long as you are professional about how you present it, will concur. Even if they don't, you can quite justifiably ask: 'What particular part of it would you suggest changing?' and then respond appropriately. Don't, however, let yourself or the process be diverted, as you will run a serious risk of being outmanoeuvred. Stick to the process!

Some of the earliest tactics the other party may use, deliberately or innocently, are covered in the next topic as we continue to look at shopping lists, how we develop and confirm theirs and ours, and the difficulties we may encounter.

Getting their shopping list . . . willingly

Some people are reluctant to ask the other party for their shopping list. There appears to be no valid reason for their reluctance, and there are significant dangers if you don't get it. So here are some ways that usually get it out without difficulty.

Just ask for it: 'I have eight items on my list which we will need to cover. What items do you have?'

Review the list obtained so far: 'OK, so we'll cover holiday pay, producivity bonus, annual leave, and sick leave. Anything else?'

Ask for additional items: 'OK, that's 10 items between us. I'd like us to consider parental leave for male staff as well. What else would you like covered?'

Write each item down: When someone is writing up a list, it encourages those present to add to it. This can be used to support the other methods. Some negotiators use a flip chart or similar to record the combined shopping list topics.

Remember you are not giving any details away when you are at this step. It is like the supermarket list (matches, biscuits, bread, apples) – just the item, not the detail.

Drawing the line . . . a conditional close

Now comes a critical point. You must get this combined list agreed to and then signed off. The reasons are simple. First, it ensures you know exactly what is going to be covered, so you can keep the whole package in mind. Second, it enables you to link items together, like service contracts with parts. Third, it avoids the problem of them introducing additional items later in the negotiation. Fourth, it avoids escalation and nibbling (Chapter 17) in the final stages. All very valid reasons!

When you have drawn out their list and, with yours, have produced a combined list, you can conditionally close it. The best way is to say: 'So if we can reach an agreement on these issues today, we will have a deal?'

- If the response is 'yes', then physically draw a line under the list. This clearly signifies that above-the-line issues are included in the negotiation, below-the-line are not.
- If the answer is 'no' or noncommittal, then revert to asking for additional items. You can say: 'OK, so what else do we need to cover in order to get a deal?'
- If they respond with 'Well, there's a few minor points, but those are the main ones' you must say 'Let's get those minor points onto the list so they can be considered as part of the overall package' and wait till they give them. When they finish, repeat the conditional close sentence again.

Cherry-picked ... to death!

What a lovely expression negotiators use – cherry-picking – for a nasty tactic! Put very crudely, cherry-picking involves one party picking all the best cherries, eating them and leaving the other party the stones. They do it by insisting that each item be dealt with separately and a decision made on it before moving on to the next item.

There's a superb Training Direct video* with Penelope Keith as a guest-house owner, with a scene showing her being cherry-picked to death by her cook, Mrs Gudgeon. The conversation goes something like ...

Penelope: 'Mrs Gudgeon, have you considered my suggestion?' (that Mrs Gudgeon do extra work in exchange for extra pay)
Mrs Gudgeon: 'Yes I have.'
Penelope: 'And what's your reaction?'
Mrs Gudgeon: 'I would require Wednesday afternoons off.'
Penelope: 'Oh, instead of Saturdays?'
Mrs Gudgeon: 'In addition to Saturdays.'
Penelope: 'Oh, I ...' (Penelope then remembers that she must be prepared to move, so she moves!)
Penelope: 'Well, I dare say something could be arranged.'
Mrs Gudgeon: 'And then there is the question of my room.'
Penelope: 'Your room?'
Mrs Gudgeon: 'It requires redecorating!'
Penelope: 'Oh, very well. Now about the extra housework ...'
Mrs Gudgeon (breaking in): 'And then there's the telly.'
Penelope: 'But I already supply you with a television set.'
Mrs Gudgeon: 'Black and white.'

And so it went on and on, related Penelope afterwards: 'I agreed to everything, I was so anxious to get it settled. But then what do you think she said?'

Mrs Gudgeon: 'And finally I should require rather more remuneration than you are offering!'

---

* 'The Art of Negotiating', a Training Direct video available from FIRST Training: New Zealand 0800 872464: Australia 1800 011 335

Penelope: 'But the business can't afford any more!'
Mrs Gudgeon: 'In that case I can't afford to take on the extra work!'

Poor Penelope! So how do we avoid that fate? The most important action by you is to insist that firm decisions are not made on any item until all have been discussed. This enables you to link items together, to change earlier suggestions if subsequent discussions changed the basis for your earlier proposal, and of course to stop the other party cherry-picking. To be fair to some sincere but unskilled negotiators, they do not realise they are cherry-picking, but that's no reason to let them do it!

You may think that cherry-picking yourself is a good idea. It can be. You may achieve more in certain areas, but the consequence may be that you fail to get the very best out of each aspect, and come away with a lopsided outcome. If as the result of your cherry-picking you get all of what you want on three variables, there may be no room left for the other party to give you anything at all on the remaining four variables. Negotiation outcomes are usually about balance – balance between the competing needs and objectives of two parties over a range of common variables and issues. So in practice the skilled negotiator avoids cherry-picking – practising and receiving it.

Straw men . . . room to move

Another strange term that you need to know – but I guess aptly described in the dictionary definition – 'a person of little substance'! And that epitomises the variables negotiators can include in a list of demands (part of the shopping list) that are not important to them, of no particular concern if they don't achieve them, but are there to give them room to move and something else to trade on. Nasty!

How do you know which are genuine variables and which are straw men? You don't, but you can apply some intelligent research, market knowledge, probing questions and plain common sense to winkle them out.

A few years ago we had a young lawyer on a seminar whose

sole job, for 40 hours every week, was to search for straw men in employment contracts. Her sole full-time job! She loved it – it brought out the detective in her. Let's have a look at how they work.

You're negotiating the next two years' rent for your business premises with the landlord. The market has moved up 5%, and while you realise that an increase of that amount is likely to be what they will want, you don't really want to pay more than 4%. So you look carefully over all the lease documents and see that the landlord is responsible for all exterior maintenance, including the car park, gardens, outbuildings, etc. Now, the car park is metalled and gets pot-holed in winter; the gardens, although maintained by an external contractor, get littered during the week from passing traffic; and the outbuildings get graffitied regularly. So you decide to insert some straw men in your shopping list.

1. Car park to be sealed. (And you have a list showing that this car park is the only one in the street that isn't sealed.)
2. Gardens to be cleared of rubbish three times a week. (Mention that the neighbouring businesses are complaining.)
3. Graffiti to be painted over within two days. (Happens on average twice a month, and other local businesses paint over theirs immediately.)
4. Rent increase to be no more than 3% given the current economic environment. (Whether it is good or bad it can always appear tough to your type of business!)

What particular demand do you think the landlord will like least? We'll guess the car park, followed by the graffiti. But you insist that these are very important; you'll stress the dangers of pot-holes in winter (has the landlord got good public liability insurance?); you'll mention that his property looks the worst in the street and is downgrading the value of the property, etc. By the time you've finished, you'll have reluctantly agreed to accept an unsealed car park for another two years, but the holes will be filled in; you've reluctantly offered to use your own staff to paint over the graffiti and pick up the rubbish in the garden during the week; and you've reluctantly agreed to a 3% increase this year moving to 4% the next. Those straw men really worked for you!

Now, don't expect that the other party will fall for your straw men, just as you will not fall for theirs. But they are a very useful tactic to use if you can justify their inclusion, and use them if needed.

To finish this topic: over a few glasses of wine in a Copenhagen hotel, two of our graduates were contemplating the next day's negotiations. They'd been at it for two days – it was a major international contract. 'What say we put in a couple of those straw men they taught us,' suggested one. 'OK,' said the other as they ordered another bottle. 'Let's go for that additional equipment in the lab, and while we're at it ask that they subsidise the first two years' research!' The next morning, quite sober and very professional, they introduced these two items into the shopping list (which was very long and the overall deal was into tens of millions). When it came time to discuss these two items, the lead negotiator on the other side read them, asked a couple of questions, and said: 'OK, they're fine. Include them in our R&D.' And that was it – $180,000 just added in! They tell me they celebrated in style that night!

Key Point Summary
- The discussion stage strongly influences the following stages
- It is process driven and follows a logical sequence of agreements
- Sequential agreements enhance the subsequent steps
- Expanded win/win outcomes rely on positive agreements, not disagreements
- The steps involve introductions, rapport and relationship building, commitment to a win/win outcome, agreement on the overall objective, the use of opening gambits, setting agendas, and developing a combined shopping list
- Good negotiators are skilled at developing and obtaining agreement on a combined shopping list that ensures all necessary items will be covered
- Good negotiators develop the combined shopping list to avoid common negative tactics being used then or later in the negotiation

▶ YOU TRY IT

Are you being cherry-picked? Decide whether the following statements involve cherry-picking, either deliberate or unintentional, by either party. Circle Yes or No. (Answers are included in the Appendix.)

❶	'I think we should cover that later.'	Yes	No
❷	'Why don't we work on that one now?'	Yes	No
❸	'We may want to consider those two items in conjunction.'	Yes	No
❹	'This one's easy – we both are happy with that.'	Yes	No
❺	'That list seems fine. Let's go through it and we'll see if anything else comes up.'	Yes	No
❻	'Let's tick that one now.'	Yes	No
❼	'My boss has a couple of minor points. We can cover them later.'	Yes	No
❽	'That one's real complicated! Let's leave it off the list at the moment.'	Yes	No
❾	'Surely we can deal with that one when we consider point six?'	Yes	No
❿	'I just hate all these lists. Why can't we just discuss and agree like professionals – we both know how far we can go on most of these!'	Yes	No

Control the process – manage the outcome

14 | Expansion – the time for creativity

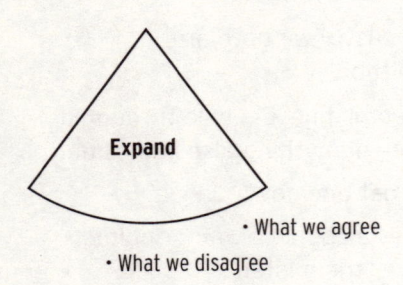

```
      ___
     /   \
    / Expand\
   /_____\
              • What we agree
         • What we disagree
```

▶As soon as the shopping list that you will work on together has been developed and confirmed, the negotiation will move into its most active stage – expansion. During this process, you will be considering every aspect of every variable in detail, and you will be relying heavily on your preparation work. In particular, you will use your settlement outcome objectives form as your principal guide.

You are there for agreement . . . so get the climate right

The first objective should be to establish and confirm the joint commitment to a win/win outcome. This will have started forming in the discussion phase, and you may not need to take any specific action for it to continue. However, positive statements by you at this step will encourage the other party to reciprocate – behaviour breeds behaviour!

Confirm those items where your discussions have indicated there is no disagreement. You cannot commit yourself to them yet, or you may leave yourself open to cherry-picking. What you can say is: 'We are in complete agreement about the make-up of these three items, so I suggest we put them aside at the moment. If nothing comes up that will disturb them then they'll stay as they are in the final agreement.'

This simple confirming of some common ground creates a feeling of joint commitment to win/win and a climate of agreement. (After all, negotiation seeks agreement, not disagreement, so why not start off that way?)

You can then move on to those items where there are differences.

Aim high! . . . stay with your optimistic objectives

Differences simply mean that your outcome objectives for that particular variable differ from theirs. It is now up to you to discuss each difference in turn, probing to identify their positions. (This does involve questioning and listening skills – a topic covered in Chapter 21.)

As you indicate your position, always open with your optimistic figure. The only time you should deviate from this at this early stage is when the preliminary discussions, such as getting out the shopping list, indicate that your preparation was incorrect. They may have revealed a factor that you were not aware of, and this has caused you to alter your range and positions within the range. This could either be up or down.

You are buying a horse for your daughter for pony club riding. The price stated is $2500, which is $800 more than similar ponies of that age and condition. But during your initial meeting with the owner, you find that its sire is well known and has consistently produced excellent riding ponies. In fact, you recall your daughter saying that her pony club instructor mentioned they were always in high demand. So you mentally up your range by the $800, and propose from there!

Or it could go the other way. You are in the middle of negotiating to buy a house which meets your requirements in every possible way, including a peep of the sea through trees in the distance. You have had it valued, and the price asked is not too far above the valuation, so you are prepared to go some way above the valuation to get it. You don't know the area very well, so you take a few minutes away from the vendor and agent to give yourself some time to think. You then spot a grove of native trees which you know are protected. You suddenly realise that these are the very trees that surround your peep of the sea. You realise that in a few years that view will have vanished! So you take out your notes (in the form of your settlement outcome objectives) and adjust your price down by the few thousand you had added in your preparation. And you know that although it is not a variable in that neither the vendor nor you can do anything about the trees and thus the gradual loss of the view, you will be able to raise it as a negative when you are justifying why you aren't prepared to pay the extra.

Research in all types and at all levels of negotiation indicates that those who maintain their high aim, their optimistic objectives, eventually settle at a higher level than those who readily move down. The simple fact is that positive and optimistic attitudes directly affect negotiations, as they affect most other competitive endeavours in life. So every text on negotiation includes the overriding mandate – aim high and maintain your aim.

As you proceed to discuss the areas of difference between you, you will begin to uncover those areas where you see room for them to move, and for you to move. This is the time to begin making tentative proposals.

Make your proposals tentative . . . use 'what if . . . then perhaps . . .'

You may well stick to your opening position as you make a proposal about a particular aspect, or you may adjust it based on your current knowledge of the situation affecting you both.

Aspects that are still based on assumptions should be checked out before any proposal is made. Say something along the lines of: 'I understand that you have recently increased your range – is that correct, or have I got the facts wrong?' or 'I've assumed that your price is based on the order being available by the end of the month – is that correct?' Never proceed without checking them out! The expression you should never have to use after the negotiation is completed is: 'Oh dear, I only wish I'd asked!'

When you make a proposal, it must be couched in tentative language and always be tagged with a condition that they do

> **Those who aim low usually hit the target.**
> **Denis Waitley & Remi L. Witt**

something in return. This is fundamental to initiating trading, even though we are only at the proposal step. Let's look at some examples to illustrate the language to use to keep it as a suggestion, tentative, for consideration.

'If I were to allow you the car on Friday nights as well as Sunday afternoons, would you consider washing the windows inside every month, as well as outside which you currently do?'

'What if I provided the timber for the fence? Could you perhaps provide the paint and share the labour cost?'

'Could you look at giving me the extra week's leave in January, provided I was able to work the Saturdays in February?'

'We could possibly arrange the packers to be finished by five, but could you manage to have your people out by 10?'

Notice the language is tentative – consider, if, what if, could, possibly, look at, perhaps.

The response to your proposals will enable you to assess, for each variable, where each of you is prepared to move. Note these possible movements on your settlement outcome objectives form – use it as your notepad. You will find it a brilliant tool when you get used to using it.

You will also note that some variables are best when linked together. In fact, many variables in a negotiation will automatically find a link, sometimes more than one. For example: packaging and delivery; amount purchased and volume price; service and usage; pocket money and household help; pay rise and productivity; quality and inspection; interest rate and type of loan; rental and length of lease.

Some multiple links include: rental, rent review, car parks, lease term, signage; advertising rate, by size, by position, by day of insertion, by numbers of insertions; freight, insurance, loading, documentation; installation, service, training, delivery.

After these steps, which you know take time but become the essential ingredients of the best deal for both parties, you can move to those areas where you have major differences or have different requirements altogether. For example, I may be negotiating the lease of a commercial building from you and have little interest in how you account for the total rental. As far as I am concerned, as long as it's at current market rates in total I don't particularly care. However, it is very important for you as landlord that the rental is structured to provide the highest value or market capitalisation. And the mix between space rental, partitioning, fixtures and fittings, air-conditioning, car parks, signage, and so on affects this figure. Provided your calculations are neutral to me (and I would get my own accountant to verify that), I will negotiate other matters and sign a lease agreement.

Search for options . . . explore, expand, explode!

Where there are differences, you will need to explore options and alternatives. Some may fall into the category of problems – that is, you both agree you have the same objective for this aspect, so it becomes a problem-solving exercise and separated out as such.

You already know how to brainstorm and create mind-maps to help creativity and expand the options. Skilled negotiators are willing to do this, as they know from experience that if a deal is going to be made, then both parties have to be involved in its development. And when there are major differences they will not be overcome by staying silent – nothing will happen! The process to this point has ensured that both parties are positive towards each other and still working towards a win/win agreement. This sharing of creativity does not mean they are giving away information that might work against them when they come to trade those final outstanding areas – far from it. They often find a whole new area of possibilities opens up during the expansion stage as both parties endeavour to come up with a range of alternatives to consider and choose from. Each are experts in their own industry and company, and the combined brainpower is significant!

The same process works equally well with family and other personal negotiations. Each party brings their own perspectives to the negotiating table. How often do you hear people say:

'I'd never thought of it that way before!' or 'That's a novel twist!' or 'Now why didn't I think of that!' or even occasionally, 'Gee, you're brilliant!'

Don't forget the two magic words that work so well – what if . . .

When you have a problem to solve jointly, use the six-step method covered in Chapter 2. It's simple and it works!

Key Point Summary
- Creativity is the foundation of the expansion stage
- Creativity relies on an open mind willing to explore options
- Creativity works on enhancing outcomes, not giving away positions
- A positive approach to exploring alternative ways increases success
- Proposals should be at the top end of the optimistic position
- Proposals are made positively but tentatively to promote expansion
- Problems can be solved by using a problem-solving process

▶YOU TRY IT

Here is a series of statements used during either the discussion or the expansion stages of negotiation. Decide which stage. (Answers are included in the Appendix.)

1. 'If we were prepared to consider that, would you look at changing your method of charging?'
2. 'I'm happy to include that on the list. But we also need to discuss the way that we handle the overseas enquiries.'
3. 'You say it's difficult to meet that timeframe. Could you, if I managed to increase the number of machines?'
4. 'Perhaps we could look at that later when we cover the extra work involved.'
5. 'We could add that in later if the extra work required it.'

6. 'Possibly. How about you review your figure on that basis, and I'll work out if we can up the numbers at our end.'

7. 'Come on Dad, it's the school holidays! You can't expect me to get through all those jobs.'

8. 'Come on Dad. The school holidays are only two weeks. However if I do complete all those jobs then I'd expect some bonus - say an extra $50.'

9. 'Yes you have a point. Let's see what options we have to get around that one.'

10. 'I know you are concerned about the increased rates, but what other issue has triggered this off? Is it the timing of the increase or perhaps the way it was initially handled?'

15 | Trading - unique to negotiation

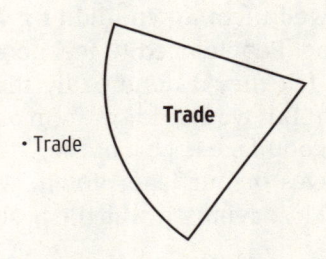

Trade
· Trade

▶Trading is a unique part of the negotiation process. It is approached by some with trepidation, by others with excitement. The reason is simple – trading or bargaining is the point where the deal is finally done, where the final exchanges of variables and positions are crystallised – fixed for the world to see! As trading is stressful for most negotiators, emotions and behaviours may become erratic and untypical. Emotional control is therefore essential and for most of us the rule 'slow down' is a saviour!

During the expansion stage the potential trades and their limits have been explored and the bargaining process links, weighs, balances and then produces the final package. The settlement outcome objectives chart is the master plan. It is important to continue a positive attitude and 'aim high' approach. Bargaining tactics are used with confidence. Like a pro golfer's clubs, each one is understood, their effect known – when, where and how to use them clear – through regular practice and use.

Now it's crunch time . . . the finality of bargaining
Trading, bargaining, exchanging, give and take – whichever term you use, in the context of negotiation the transaction is

the same. You give me something of what I want, and I will give you something of what you want – trading worth for worth, variable for variable, item for item, until agreement on the exchange is reached.

Listening to people talk about their 'successful' negotiations, you would think that negotiation equals trading. They talk with animation about how much they achieved by giving away so little, how they did a great deal, got more than they could have hoped, screwed them down, didn't give anything away, etc! And that's fine. People need to feel good about the deals they do – if they felt they'd done badly they may not be so willing to try again! But we also know from our own experience that putting on a good face is part of the deal too – even if we feel we let ourselves or our team down, we will justify the outcome achieved by saying: 'It was the best I could get in the circumstances.'

Now, the truth of the matter is that trading is not the whole of negotiation – trading is a step within the process of a negotiation. Negotiation includes preparation, then discussion to see what may be needed to trade, then a creative look at possible alternative ways of achieving the same outcome; then – and only then – trading those aspects where earlier agreement has not been reached. And research on business negotiations would suggest that the actual trading time in a face-to-face negotiation (from the beginning of the discussion stage to the point of final agreement) ranges between ten and thirty per cent. So don't think that you have to be a 'born trader' to do a good deal! It helps to have a 'feel' for trading, but the best deals, certainly the ones that involve long-term relationships, are done by ordinary people who understand the total process and prepare themselves accordingly.

We find in our seminars that those who come in as 'wheeler-dealers' rarely get the best deals in the case-studies. Their main fault is rushing into the trading step – they have the mistaken belief that everything has to be traded! But we know from experience that thoughtful discussion prior to that step will ensure that what and how we trade will be the best in terms of our outcome objectives, for both parties. Success in trading is directly related to what we have done up to that point.

Our objective when trading is very important – to trade variables within the settlement ranges we set, or have since modified, at the point closest to our opening or optimistic settlement positions, or higher. If you keep that objective firmly fixed in your mind during the trading, you will achieve more of what you want, without negating your win/win approach. You will be in no danger of breaching your bottom line, and the overall agreement will satisfy you emotionally as well as in material terms.

But as the heading says, bargaining is crunch time! So let's take a look at how we should firm up those tentative proposals we made earlier.

'If . . . then . . .'

The language we use when trading is important – it should firm up previous suggested exchanges and proposed actions. We are offering or seeking final commitment, so tentative words or phrases are inappropriate.

The two most useful words, and ones you should commit to heart, are 'if' and 'then'. But – and this is vital – they must go together. Trading is about give and take, not give by itself! So put them together into 'if . . . then . . .'

You will also convert those proposal words such as 'could you' into 'will you' or even 'you will'. 'Perhaps' and 'maybe' are no longer used! Let's look at some examples of words and phrases that are useful when trading. First, when there is a possibility of modification:

'If we arrange the transport, then your people will look after the unloading. How's that?'

'OK, how about this – I supervise the team during training sessions, then you do the workout before the game and referee. Agreed?'

'How's this for a solution? If I get the figures to you by the end of the month, then will you agree to start the launch by the 15th?'

'If you agree to work that extra hour in the morning, then I'll agree to the bonus at the original amount. Will you do that?'

Note that these firm up previous proposals, or suggest

something close. Agreement from the other party is still sought, and there is room for change if either side wish. But once they agree, they become commitments that form part of the final agreement.

Now some examples where tentative agreement was reached earlier, and the phrases are used to get the final OK.

'We seem clear on the transport. You will do the paperwork on Friday, and I will load the truck Saturday morning. Agreed?'

'Right, let's get this clear. I pay by the 12th, you include the cover. Correct?'

'So . . . you will provide the executive suite, provided we stay the three nights. When do you want my payment?'

You'll soon become proficient in these. Just keep in mind what you are wanting to achieve – agreement, commitment, action.

Keep your objectives in mind . . . it's the package that counts

Remember ranking your variables into aces, fillers, swaps and no-no's? How could you forget! And their ranking has been staring at you as you've used your settlement outcome objectives form as your guide throughout the negotiation. Now is the time that those variables involved in trading really work for you. Before you start trading on them, however, check that the rank you gave them is still correct. Some information gained during the negotiation so far may have changed your earlier perception. For example, something that you thought was an ace for you isn't – in fact it may not even be a filler! On the other hand, a swap may now be an ace. So take a few moments to collect your thoughts and check your rankings before you commit to any trade.

You'll also recall breaking the variables into small units. This greatly assists your ability to trade, as you are able to mix-and-match a number of components within one variable category without adversely affecting the overall outcome for that issue or topic.

Delivery is the issue or topic. As such it is not variable – it is the aspects of delivery that are the variables. The variables derived from delivery would include time of, urgent service, where pick-up, where deliver, methods of payment for, return policy, insurance on, phone service, door-to-door, overnight, international, tracking service, etc.

Being able to trade on each of these gives you a high degree of flexibility. But you can also group them together if that is more appropriate for a particular negotiation. For example, your 'standard' delivery service may be all that is needed by one customer, whereas another may want special arrangements on every aspect.

What you must keep in mind is the whole package. You trade on each item individually on the basis of cost to you and value to them – that is how you ranked them and how you must trade them. You can link variables together where relevant, but keep in mind you have a bottom line for each. Do not go beyond that – ever. (If you do, your initial analysis is questionable – unless subsequent information indicates your assessment was incorrect due to lack of information.)

It is the overall balance at the end that you will be judged on – whether by yourself or others. And the objectives are the criteria against which judgement is made.

Fools rush in . . . take time to think!

It is normal to feel stressed and pressured when negotiating, and the worst time for most of us is when trading. Preparation is fine. Discussion puts us under some pressure, but if our communication skills are good then we usually enjoy getting to know people and obtaining information. The expansion stage can be daunting for some, though once they've had a taste of creative thinking and problem-solving in a process-driven way, they come to appreciate its worth. But trading – that does cause trepidation for many of us. Measure pulse rates – they're up. And there's the problem!

When we are under pressure or stressed we are not always fully in control of our actions. Emotions run high. The mind

> If you can't stand the heat, stay out of the kitchen. **Harry S. Truman**

panics. We want it to end quickly. We find ourselves prepared to give things away just to finish it. We rush our calculations. We adopt an 'it'll be all right' attitude. Put bluntly, we are out of control!

So this is the time to be most vigilant, most disciplined. And there is one basic, simple universal rule – slow down. Probably the two words we hear most often from graduates when they report successful negotiations – they 'slowed down'! How?

- Ask for a short break: 'I need a two-minute stretch. Now seems a good time. OK?' and stand up and move.
- Ask for a glass of water: 'I'm thirsty. I'll get a glass of water' or 'It's stuffy in here, and I'm getting dehydrated. I need some water.' Stand up and move.
- Ask for a refreshment break: 'It's over an hour since we broke, and I'm needing some sustenance! Let's have a five-minute break.' Stand up and move.
- Go to the restroom: 'I require a short break to visit the restroom. We should break for three minutes.' Stand up and go.
- Ask for a short recess: 'I need to calculate the effect of that request. I require 10 minutes. I suggest we take a 15-minute break now.' Stand up.
- Take notes: While you don't need to say anything, the fact that you are taking notes often causes others to slow down – they don't want you to miss anything they say!

However, to slow it down you can just say: 'Would you please just hold it there? I'm getting those points down to ensure I cover them for you in that order later.' And write even more slowly!

You will come up with ways to slow it down that suit you. The main point to remember is that you must be in control at all times, and the moment you feel out of control take some positive action.

That statistic mentioned earlier about time – 80% of the value traded during a negotiation occurs in the last 20% of the time – now has relevance!

Tips for trading . . . some bargaining tactics

The following suggestions are for you to study. They are a collection of bargaining tactics that negotiators use to ensure their trading is effective. Some are offensive, as they are proactive moves. They should not offend! Others are defensive – tactics to minimise aggressive moves by the other party. Most are neutral in terms of a win/win mentality – they are simply used to ensure trading objectives are met or exceeded.

1. Always, always 'tag' your offers.
'We will supply the labour, if you provide the machines.'
    'I'd be happy to work on Friday, if you do my shift on Sunday.'
    'You can have the van for your skiing trip, as long as you help with the shift next weekend.'

2. Always, always trade on the basis of value to them, cost to you.
High value to them, low cost to you. Value everything in the light of what it is worth to the other party.

3. Always, always trade your variables – never donate.
A donation is a give-away, and may not be seen as having value. We do free attitude and leadership training for schools. If we think the perception of the value of the training might be low because it is free, we often make a charge and then give it back in the form of some tangible item the school needs, such as music stands for the orchestra. And remember that children need to learn a sense of value, so get into the habit of trading value with them too.

4. Always, always build the value of the aspects you are trading.
Never give them away, and don't trade them too quickly or you will lower their perceived value. If we get something too easily in a negotiation we get suspicious – what have we missed?

5. Always, always build their emotional satisfaction.
Feelings are often more important and have more real value than the material outcomes. And 'bragging' rights are important for anyone who has to report on the outcome to someone else

– a partner, a colleague, a boss. Send them away so they can brag!

'Well Kathy, that was a tough negotiation, one of the toughest I've had. But I did a great deal when you consider how difficult the market is at the moment, and I didn't have to give away the total rebate.'

6. Always, always keep a record of your progress – on your settlement outcome objectives form is best.
This way you always know what you have discussed, what has been proposed, what agreed, and what is still left to trade. It also keeps you firmly in control – whether or not you are leading the trading process, or being a very thoughtful follower!

And notes are essential when you're summarising and finalising agreements and action steps.

7. Always, always keep your movements small.
Break your variables into small units. A reduction of $1000 can be broken down into two of $500, or 10 of $100. You can get a return on each, so don't be over-generous!

8. Always, always indicate you are running out!
As well as breaking your variables into smaller units, make each trade progressively smaller. For example, the $1000 could be traded as a $500, then a $300, then a $100, then a $50, etc. What signal are you sending? 'I'm running out on this one!' The worst thing you could signal would be the other way – they might come to expect your next trade would be $2000!

9. Always, always slow down or take a break if you get into a panic or don't understand something.
Never respond to pressure with hasty actions or decisions. Better to lose a small amount of face than a large amount of bottom line!

10. Always, always keep your creative mind open.
Keep asking, aloud or silently, those two magic words – 'what if'. As much as anything else, they'll keep you alert during what is for most of us the difficult and pressured part of a negotiation. It is never too late to expand the outcome!

11. Always, always be on the lookout for straw men.
You may have picked up one or more during the earlier stages, but it is in the trading that they are finally used. So test them out – check their relative importance by offering a trade with, say, a filler of yours. Or just call their bluff if you are sure it is a straw man; you really have nothing to lose.

12. Always, always review their new demands in the light of your previous trades.
While the shopping list that you agreed on at the end of the discussion stage should avoid any 'extra' requests, many negotiators will try to add something in later on! It may be innocent, something they really did forget, but never give way on it. Trade something.

'That request you've just sprung on me causes me concern. A few minutes ago I agreed to run that extra line for you over a weekend, but that was on the basis of our quoted volume. You are now proposing that we increase the volume by 10% – but it's not as simple as that for production. If you want the extra, then it will cost an extra late-night shift. Are you prepared to pay for that?'

Also refer to nibbling and escalation in Chapter 16.

13. Always, always express money in terms that look and sound the best in the particular situation.
Car finance repayments are always quoted as per week – if they quoted them per month many people would not buy! Most appliance retailers use weekly figures. Your mortgage is usually quoted monthly. Most of us don't bother to multiply it by 12 and then by the number of years! And large ticket items are almost always expressed just below the zeros – cars and boats are $29,995 rather than $30,000!

And if you use percentages, think about whether you should talk in percentage terms or the absolute figure. Which sounds more, 10% or $100 on a $1000 price? What about 15% or $7,500 on a $50,000 price? I think I'd prefer the $7,500!

If you are dealing in foreign currencies, use precise conversions, not guesstimates. Small percentage or point differences can make or break a bottom line.

Trading – unique to negotiation | 143

14. Always, always have an escape route if your final offer is not your final offer!
When you make a final offer, you are putting your credibility on the line. If the other party rejects your final offer, or offers you some alternative, and you have to change yours, unless you can provide a valid reason for changing you will lose credibility.

I recall one negotiation where the rate of interest was a variable. The lender stated: '15% is the best I can do'. After a couple of minutes of persuasion by the borrower, the lender was heard to say: 'Well, 14% is my final offer.' A few minutes later, after some heated argument, the lender rather resignedly said: 'I can't possibly go below 13% – that's my final offer.' I noted the final deal went through at 12%!

So if you do say: 'That's my final offer,' either stick to it or have some way of trading yourself out of a credibility gap!

15. Always, always mask your discretionary authority.
If you have the discretion to give things away, which may be monetary or other resources like time, don't tell the other party. What is likely to happen if you proudly say: 'I'm important – I can give you an extra . . .'? Stupid? Of course, but you'd be surprised how many people unwittingly give away such vital information. Be on your guard when questions about your authority or limits are raised.

Finally, remember that trading is definitely crunch time – when all the work to this point is brought together and a consolidated package of variables is merged and agreed. It is this package that the future actions and relationships are based on. It can be scary. It is the time when most of us feel under pressure, and we are often tired. Don't let tiredness rob you of your wits, or push you into giving things away just to get the deal over with. Stick to the process, follow the trading rules and these bargaining tips, and you will end up with a win/win deal that you will be proud to brag about!

Key Point Summary
- In negotiation the terms trading and bargaining are synonymous
- Trading or bargaining is one stage in the negotiation process
- Bargaining takes up a relatively small part of the negotiation time
- The aim when trading is to achieve our optimistic positions
- We may achieve above, at or below our optimistic positions
- Final settlement points are a direct result of all prior steps
- Trading is based on the positions, priorities and rankings set out in the settlement outcome objectives chart
- Variables are traded individually or linked where appropriate
- Bargaining phrases firm up previous tentative proposals
- Bargaining is stressful, and whether positive or negative emotional control is required
- When trading is completed a deal has been agreed

▶TRY IT OUT
Score yourself on the checklist on page 146 – how effective are your list of some bargaining behaviours? Rate yourself. (Comments on these behaviours are included in the Appendix.)

	Almost always	Often	Some-times	Seldom	Almost never
1. I pause and think before responding to an offer					
2. I analyse and cost a trade before accepting					
3. I use my aces to gain maximum possible return					
4. I use a written format to map out the variables					
5. I adjourn or caucus when I feel the need					
6. I have a store of ways to get a short break					
7. I keep track of progress in writing					
8. I use fillers to encourage movement					
9. I slow down if I feel pressured or panic					
10. I continue to aim high throughout					
11. I control my body language however I feel					
12. I ask questions if I do not understand something					
13. I keep in mind the whole package					
14. I treat every constant as a possible variable					
15. I tag every offer I make					
16. I keep my movements small					
17. I make notes about possible straw men					
18. I resist any attempt at them nibbling					
19. I keep my authority limits and discretions private					
20. I find the bargaining step stressful					
Total ✓	×5	×4	×3	×2	×1
Total/100					

16 | Finalising – putting the deal to bed

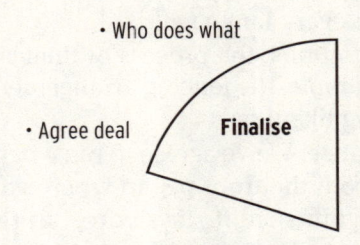

- Who does what
- Agree deal
- **Finalise**

▶When the trading is completed the negotiation can be finalised. One party takes the initiative by summarising the individual and combined points of settlement and agreements, and asks the other for confirmation that the total arrangement is acceptable. A positive decision signifies final agreement. All negotiations require some form of follow up. Simple or regular negotiations may need only verbal agreement about who does what when; complex negotiations invariably need written and formal documentation to record the various outcomes and respective responsibilities. The negotiation at this point has brought the parties to an agreement – the task is now one of putting it into effect to ensure each party is committed and actually achieves their objectives.

Getting agreement . . . and complete commitment
Asking people to commit to something is difficult for many people – so if you're in that category you are very normal. In fact, we often get requests from sales managers who say: 'My salespeople aren't closing. Help!' What they are really saying is: 'My salespeople are not recognising when their customer is

ready to buy, and when they do recognise it, they are not sufficiently confident or competent enough to ask.' So let's look at the topic of getting agreement.

First, recognising the signals. In simple transactions, like doing a deal with your partner over the weekend activities, the signals are pretty clear. At the end of the trading, one party is going to say: 'OK, I'm happy to go along with that. When do we head off?' That only leaves the other party one option: 'Tomorrow morning straight after breakfast.' And the deal is done, or 'closed' in selling terminology; 'finalised' in negotiation language; 'agreement' in every language!

In more detailed negotiations, the process of finalising may take a little longer. For example, the fencing arrangement might conclude after the trading like this:

'OK Henry, let's summarise. We've agreed to run a new paling fence on the boundary from the front peg to where your shed starts. From the back of your shed it stays wire, but replaced. You provide the concrete mixer, cement and new mesh. I provide the palings and paint. We share all other materials costs 50-50, and we do it ourselves, on Saturday mornings, starting next week. Is that what we've agreed?'

'Yep, that sounds pretty good by me, Colin. Let's do it!'

'Righto, Henry – let's shake on that. I'm really going to enjoy working on this, and it will certainly make a big difference to our shrubs out the front. All we need to do now is order in . . .'

Note that Colin took the initiative for the finalising. He summarised the result of the trading, confirmed that he had it right, and then 'closed' the deal – or finalised the arrangements – by asking for a handshake (an almost universal method of agreeing to a deal).

In complex negotiations, there will be a whole series of summaries. Each will be agreed to separately, as a small parcel within a greater package. Each 'parcel' needs to be signed off, which may be a simple: 'Yes, we're agreed on that one,' through to a formally written point-by-point agreement on each.

If you are interested in further reading about the subject of closing, there are many books on selling which cover it fully. There are various techniques for closing – we include them in our sales seminars, as they are designed to help people make buying decisions that meet their needs.

From our experience as negotiation trainers and observers of actual business negotiations, however, we find that anyone who follows the negotiation process, has a reasonable level of observation and communication skills, and can summarise after trading is completed does not need to worry about closing techniques. To the sincere negotiator, finalising becomes a step in the process and is as natural as starting the process off. So practise finalising by summarising some of your more simple negotiations, and you will find the more complex ones fit the same pattern. You may have to repeat the summary process several times though!

Watch out for nibblers . . . and escalators

There are two tactics, introduced in the last chapter, which may occur during the finalising stage. Nibbling and escalation may be deliberate tactics, or innocently introduced. We need to manage them.

Nibbling

Nibbling is the practice of taking small repeated bites from a variable. 'Just a little bit more' is the nibbler's approach. Because they are such small bites, and presented very reasonably, the tendency is to give them away as a gesture of goodwill. Don't! Nibbles are very bad for your bottom line! (Or should we say waste-line!) The rule in trading is never donate, always tag offers with a condition. So if you have a nibbler who wants that little bit extra, ask for something in return. For example: 'Beth, can you fit just one extra on to that first consignment? It would make the second one easier for both of us.'

Your response should be: 'I could consider that, Gavin, but it's likely to cause a delay at the terminal. How about you agreeing to an extra handling fee if I can organise it?'

Now the ball is back in Gavin's court – Beth has agreed to consider it, but only on the condition that Gavin pays for it. If Gavin is serious, he will agree to the extra fee or negotiate on it; if he was nibbling, or it was a straw man, he will leave it by saying: 'We may not need to, so I'll come back to you on that.' Beth has not only successfully diverted a nibble, but she has sent Gavin a message: 'If you try nibbling, I'll call your bluff.' And she has avoided setting a precedent. If she had allowed it, you can be sure it would be taken for granted by Gavin in future, and built in to his list of demands as a given.

Escalation

Escalation is the second tactic used in the finalising stage. Again, it may be innocent or deliberate. And again, it must be firmly resisted. Escalation occurs after agreement on a variable or set of variables. For example:

You have completed summarising all aspects of the negotiation, got agreement on all, and are ready to leave. As you are completing the courtesies of leaving, Joy, the other party, says: 'Oh, Martyn, there's one little thing you could do for me. I know we agreed that Sally would be our nominee for the conference, but it would be really useful if Jan could be there as well. I know that's a bit extra for you but, after all, they can share a room, and having them both there will be beneficial to us both.'

Now to us as listeners we may find that very plausible and reasonable, and would probably say to Martyn: 'Yes, why not? A good idea!' But Martyn knows that having one extra person there from Joy's company is not as easy as it sounds. There would be significant extra costs, as the hotel arrangement is based on the numbers, not the rooms. Groups have already been selected, and any additional people would upset the balance. It was Joy's request in the first place that they only nominate one, and that condition was built into the budget and the total deal. So Martyn replies:

'At this late stage that may not be wise, as the group selection has been made on the basis of one only, and an extra machine and instructor might have to be brought in. Would you be prepared to meet some of the extra costs? Otherwise it would be over budget, and I would have to renegotiate that part of the arrangement with you.'

Martyn has put the ball into Joy's court. If she is serious about Jan's attendance, she will agree to renegotiate that part of the deal. If it was a deliberate attempt at escalation, and she is not prepared to wear the consequences of extra cost, she will extricate herself by saying: 'Oh, I didn't realise that the numbers were so fixed, so we'll leave it as Sally only. Perhaps we could look at Jan another time.'

Martyn has successfully defused an escalation attempt, avoided setting a precedent, and like the example on nibbling, clearly signalled to Joy that he will not be escalated upon.

If you have to deal with nibblers and escalators, be assertive but remain polite and professional. If they have done it innocently, you don't want to offend them; if done deliberately, you want them to know you know what they attempted, but let them save face. You don't need enemies in negotiation!

The deal's not done . . . until the paperwork is finished!

Even with your children, it's not a bad idea to write down those things you've agreed on, and pin them up where everyone can see them. It keeps everyone honest!

Obviously it's essential in every other negotiation to keep some record of what was agreed, who is responsible for what, etc. We developed for our graduates a record of agreement form, and Figure 34 shows how you can use this. For simple negotiations you may not want to go to this formality, but for major or complex negotiations you must completely record all agreements.

RECORD OF AGREEMENT

Variable	Details agreed	Action required	Who	When	Remarks

Figure 34: Record of agreement

Following major negotiations, paperwork of some sort is

almost always required. We suggest you take the initiative, as it gives you control over the time, style and content of the documentation. One international negotiator we know has a designated person in the negotiation meeting to record all proceedings, and at the end of each day a full summary of the issues discussed is prepared and delivered by mid-evening to all parties involved. It is used as a starting point summary when the negotiation resumes the next morning.

You should also take the initiative in organising the formal documentation – legal terms and conditions, heads of agreement, contracts, deeds, etc. You do not have to do it yourself – but be responsible to see that it happens.

> Coming together is a beginning;
> Keeping together is progress;
> Working together is success. **Henry Ford**

Keep it on track ... don't let it derail

From long experience debriefing negotiators in the business world, we've found that effective management of the process after the actual deal is concluded will ensure that the spirit and intent of the arrangement is carried out by all parties involved.

In buying and selling, there's a term called buyer's, or seller's, remorse. It refers to the period immediately following the signing of a deal when either, or both, parties start to worry about the deal – have they done the right thing, did they cover everything, were they cheated in any way, could they have got a better deal, what hidden agendas were there, etc. Negotiation is no different. Negotiators can feel remorseful too!

The time you are likely to strike emotional reactions, attempts at reneging and general niggles is during this period. So follow these vital steps after you've attended to the paperwork:

- Debrief within your own organisation, be it family or business.
- Ensure that what you said you would do has been done, or is being done.

- Confer with the other party – is everything on schedule, did they receive the documentation, are there any matters needing clarification, etc.
- Set up an internal system that manages the actions required by you.
- Discuss and agree on, and if required set up, a communication process between you and the other party that will ensure each is kept fully informed about the progress of the deal, whether positive or negative.

These steps apply to any negotiation – not just the complex or major ones!

Key Point Summary
- Closing down or finalising the negotiation follows the completion of bargaining
- Finalising involves summarising and gaining joint agreement
- Good negotiators take the initiative in finalising
- A record of agreement is prepared
- Action steps and responsibilities are agreed
- A follow up procedure is agreed
- Both parties proactively ensure the intent of the agreement is achieved
- Both parties proactively work to enhance the relationship

▶YOU TRY IT
How would you deal with these nibblers? Write a suitable response. (Suggested responses are included in the Appendix.)

1. 'How about an extra couple of dollars an hour for that last day I've agreed to?'
2. 'Could we just add one or two to that first load – it would make my job easier?'
3. 'Mum suggested Mark could stay as well. That'd be all right with you wouldn't it?'
4. 'I almost forgot! We need that last truck by ten o'clock. Guess that's OK?'
5. 'Would it matter to you if I kept it for another day? I'll return it Friday evening.'

17 | When in difficulties

▶The best laid plans of mice and men . . . nothing ever seems to go exactly to plan, and negotiation is no exception. Whether we like it or not, we are going to come across difficult situations, aggravating people, power plays, withheld information, etc, many of which will mean our negotiation skills are tested to the limit. Some of the negative aspects which arise within a negotiation have been covered in earlier topics. A few, however, are best dealt with separately, as they can occur at any time. Let's have a look at the main ones.

Hidden agenda

A hidden agenda may never be revealed. The other party may conceal it within any of their issues, and you may inadvertently satisfy it without them having it exposed. That may not necessarily be negative, as the aspect may have been of little or no concern to you.

As in most situations where there are two or more parties, communication between them is only as good as their skills in sending and receiving messages, both verbal and non-verbal. A skilful questioner will be better placed to bring out a hidden agenda than someone who relies solely on what is presented (Chapter 22 has some communication tips).

Although you should follow the next process in every instance, if you suspect a hidden agenda, be particularly disciplined with it. As you develop and confirm the shopping list with them, ask questions that probe why particular items are included, and link related items. If you want issues raised that they have not, then ask the reason. Be assertive when you conditionally close the list, giving clear messages that no more items will be accepted, and ensure you physically sign if off.

If a hidden agenda item is exposed at some later stage, treat it as you would a nibble or escalation.

Stall

A stall is a delaying tactic. It may be used to delay discussion or decision on a particular issue. It may be used to evade an issue altogether. Your responsibility is to find out why they are stalling. It's always useful to put yourself in their shoes for a moment, and ask yourself: 'If I was them, why would I be avoiding or delaying on this issue now?' If that doesn't shed any light, then you can probe. You can use standard information-gathering questions:

- 'This issue seems to be causing you some thought. What particular aspect is causing the problem?'
- 'You seem reluctant to move off this one. What other information would help?'
- 'This appears to be a problematic issue for you. If we took a short break, would that be useful?'
- 'There seems to be an unresolved issue here. Suppose we go over the details again, would that help?'

Their responses should indicate why they are avoiding the issue, or give you more information about their stall. Although some negotiators use stalling in a negative way (to ruffle your composure, to test your reactions to pressure, etc), it could simply be that they don't want to go any further with that issue at that point. It could be beyond their personal authority, but they don't want to admit that to you. Maybe they didn't do their homework fully and are caught out, or they're just out of their comfort zone.

So treat it matter-of-factly, and use questions to uncover the real reason, or move it on.

'Minor point'

If the words 'a few minor points' are ever used in a negotiation, your blood should run cold. What's minor? To you it might be $1000; to me $100. Everything is relative. This phrase is most likely to be used when you are closing off the shopping lists. They say something like: 'Yes, those are the main items we

> A certain amount of opposition is a great help to man. Kites rise against, not with the wind. **John Neal**

need to cover. Subject to a few minor points, if we can get agreement on those, we'll be in business!'

Your response must be: 'Well, let's get those minor points on the list as well, shall we? After all, we're looking at a total package here, and it may well be that some of those minor points can be linked in with these other items. What particular points were you thinking of?' (And then physically put your pen on the paper poised to write!)

Conditionally close the shopping list and physically draw the line across the bottom. Any points, major or minor, they might bring up later can be treated as 'below-the-line', and whether they are considered and how they are treated is up to you. They are like a nibble!

Impasse and deadlock

When a situation occurs which blocks progress, it is called an impasse. A deadlock is a state of affairs in which further action between the two parties is impossible.

Impasse

Because an impasse only relates to one situation, it is relatively easy to get around it. View it as a temporary block impeding your progress down one line, but with other lines open for you to get past, bypass it and come back to it later.

For example, you and your family are negotiating the activities for the coming weekend. You are happy to play tenpin and then go to the big game, but want to go for sushi afterwards. The children are thrilled with the tenpin, comfortable with the big game, but definitely don't want sushi. They want burgers! You've got a potential agreement on tenpin and the game, but an impasse looms on the meal arrangements. Now if either side digs their toes in, there may not be any family activity! You may decide to go to the game, with sushi afterwards, and let the children fend for themselves, ungrateful little . . .! But reason prevails as one of the children suggests a way out of the impasse. 'How about you drop us off at the burger place near the cinema, and we'll go and see that new film you're not interested in and have burgers, while you two can go to that new sushi restaurant and enjoy a lovely long meal without us hanging around!' Impasse averted, everyone happy. Impasses are like that – a little bit of creativity on someone's part, and the negotiation is back on track.

Now, it's not always going to be as simple as that obviously. So what else can you do to bypass the block? Use something along these lines:

'We seem to be stuck on that issue. What say we leave it for the moment, have a look at the next point, and then come back to it?'

'We appear to have reached an impasse on that particular topic. Would it help if we looked at it in conjunction with the next item? They both involve the northern branches and there may be a way of combining them.'

'I think we may be able to help on this one. You can't budge because your quality system would be jeopardised. And we can't move either because of the time factor in our existing contract. But if we were able to persuade our production people to increase their output in the next month, we may be able to shift our deadline. If we did that your system would not be affected. Would that get round the block?' (Note a filler has been used – low cost to you as your production manager has already indicated an increased output was scheduled; and this could remove the problem for the other party.)

Deadlocks

Deadlocks are quite different – a full stop! The negotiation process will not move forward, and all possibilities for movement have been exhausted. The parties will have to agree on the causes of the deadlock and adjourn to consider their positions. If they are unable to adjust in any way, the negotiation remains deadlocked and will need to be treated as a no-deal outcome.

Usually, however, one or both parties, during the

adjournment, are able to find some movement, and this is proposed as a way to restart the negotiation process. If the deadlock is the result of an incompatibility between people (such as a personality clash resulting in refusal to communicate), then the negotiators should be changed. A breakdown for this reason may be restarted by using a mediator, or by changing the make-up of the negotiation teams.

A deadlock need not be confrontational. It may be that as the parties move through the discussion phase, they find there are no areas of apparent agreement. They may not get as far as deadlock – but agree that a no-deal will be the only possible outcome.

Bluff

A bluff is used in two situations:
- One party pretends to be confident about an uncertain issue in order to influence the other party.
- One party deliberately sets up a deception intended to create the impression of a stronger position than they actually have.

Let's look at how these are used in a negotiation, and how their bluff may be called!

Bluffer: 'I heard that your company will be looking to upgrade to digital technology in the next few months. That should be an exciting development for you. If it is likely to happen before your financial year ends, I could set up a meeting for you with our technical whiz-kids – they could keep you continually updated.' (Bluff words: heard, looking, few, exciting, likely, whiz-kids, continually.)

Response: 'Thanks for the offer, but our headquarters has got a team already working on it. Did they mention that we were considering sourcing from Japan?' (The headquarters team and Japan may be fictional. The response is intended to see how much, if anything, the bluffer knows.)

Bluffer: 'We are likely to secure a major contract with an overseas customer shortly, which will mean our orders from you will increase significantly over the next few months. We'd expect to be on your VIP terms, so we should start that system from next month.' (Bluff words: likely, shortly, significantly, few, expect.)

Response: 'I'm very pleased to hear that. If you write me a note setting out the details of the contract and the start date, we can discuss the likely impact on us both and schedule in the VIP terms.' (Clear request for facts: contract details, date, size of order. VIP terms can wait!)

Either type of bluff can occur at any stage of the negotiation. Your knowledge of your own organisation, the competition, the other party, and your overall preparation will improve your chances of picking a bluff for what it is, and calling theirs!

Intimidation

In negotiation, intimidation is used to influence the other party's behaviour through fear. The fear may be induced by a variety of tactics, including threats, scaring, coercion, bullying, pressure and arm-twisting.

Intimidation is only successful if the recipient is willing to be threatened, scared, coerced, bullied, pressured or have their arm twisted! So your best defence against the intimidator is to assertively decline. Some responses could be:

'I have listened very carefully to what you have said. However, company policy does not allow me to divulge that information, so if you insist on having it now, we will have to adjourn for me to take advice on it.'

'I would not be able to sanction that payment, as all cash disbursements are personally signed by our controller. And no advance payments can be authorised until work has commenced. I can raise the matter with our external auditor who sets these policies if you wish.'

'It would certainly be great to be able to do it that way! I only wish I could. Perhaps you could talk to our CEO direct. I know he has very fixed views on that subject. You might be able to change them! Would you like me to arrange a meeting?'

In each of these situations, the response is designed to show the intimidator that their tactic has no effect on the recipient personally, but that they have registered the attempt. The response then turns the intimidation back to the initiator, who is placed in a position that would be untenable, and therefore they must back off. (Would they really want to adjourn, get an external auditor involved, or confront your CEO?)

To finish this discussion on a more positive note, intimidation can indeed be used in a positive and win/win way! After all, how do you coerce your partner into taking a weekend away with you? Of course you threaten them – you won't do the books, you'll renege on the parents' visit, you'll delay the painting, etc. You influence their behaviour through fear!

And when a business negotiation is getting bogged down by a stubborn person from the other side, you are quite at liberty to threaten them with: 'Bruce, if you keep insisting on that specific schedule I'm going to up the handling fees by 50%. Your boss won't like that one little bit! So make up your mind, or I'll phone the office and do it now!'

18 | Power

Sources of power... which do you have?
There are whole books about this topic! We can restrict our consideration to the sources of power that people acquire and bring to a negotiation, and how they use that power.

Let's first define what we mean by power in the negotiation situation. It's the ability to do something. It is control or a position of control. It exercises influence or authority. It may be a specific ability, capacity or faculty. Put these into a negotiation where each side has some or all of these attributes to differing levels, and you have a powerful mix. Sometimes explosive!

But in most negotiations, power is appropriately used by the owner to promote their cause, and is not used in a heavy-handed or malicious way. If we were studying political or international negotiations, we would see consistent and heavy use of power. But we are considering normal and regular negotiations in personal, social and business situations, and we need to understand how power works within those.

We derive our power base from three main sources: position, decision and personal power. You may have one, two, or all three in varying degrees.

Position power is often referred to as status power, as the power is sourced from the position that person holds at that time. Parents have position or status power over their children, and to an extent over what happens to their children, such as education. But in another environment, say at work, that position power does not exist and cannot be used. (It may become personal power at work, for example in a discussion about the problems with teenagers, but it is only position power when used in the parenting environment.)

At work we have positions, and with those positions comes the control and influence attached to them. These are typically based on a hierarchical structure, and confer status on the person in that position. For example, the chief executive is deferred to, not necessarily because people respect them, but because that position demands respect. With that position come the benefits attached to it – larger office, better car, higher remuneration, etc. The size of the organisation and type of industry may be factors. The same applies in the family situation – the parents get the choice of room they sleep in, the car they use, sometimes even their favourite chair or place at the table! The eldest child often has greater privileges based solely on their position in the family hierarchy.

The power, however, is with the position and is not permanently attached to the person. When the eldest child leaves home, the privileges may go to the next child, who now assumes the position of the eldest at home. When the chief executive retires, they leave behind their positional power. Many people who leave the position that gave them status mourn the loss – they are no longer Gill Thomas, chief executive of Growthcorp, but just Gill Thomas. Many cling to their old titles as a vestige of the power they once had, as if they would vanish without it. And many do die – literally.

Position power is real – that is, when you are in that position you have it. It cannot be taken away from the position.

Decision power gives the owner the ability to make decisions that affect others, to give or withhold resources. People with decision power can delay or withhold decisions. They can grant favours. No wonder we defer to those who have the power to make decisions that affect us! But their power is only effective when it relates to the issue affecting us. Their power may disappear as soon as the decision is made.

Decision power is essential to negotiators. Although position power is useful, without decision power they will not be able to make decisions or confirm agreements. Quite simply, the negotiation process would break down! Therefore, when people prepare for a negotiation they ensure they have the necessary decision power, or they arrange for it to be delegated to them for the period of the negotiation. They are often given specific discretions (discretionary authority) or limits (limited authority) within which they can make on-the-spot decisions during the negotiation.

Decision power is part real and part perceived. For example, the manager of a division of a large company has certain decision powers, based on the position. They may have additional decision powers – which have no relevance to the position – based on specialist expertise. When I headed the personal banking division of a large financial services group, I had high position power and some high decision power. But many of the managers who reported to me had far higher discretionary authority than me, based on their specialist knowledge and expertise. Most executives delegate decision-making down to the most appropriate level. So it is quite easy for one party in a negotiation to make assumptions about the decision power the other may have, based on a perception of what they think that person's position would warrant.

So you need to check out the decision-making authority of the other party when making agreements over negotiation variables and issues. Often a simple 'Is there anyone else we need to include in these discussions for us to be able to make final decisions and agreements today?' is sufficient to confirm their level of authority.

Personal power rests with the individual. In a negotiation situation it is arguably the most influential power. It relates to the person's knowledge, understanding of the issues involved and the other party's situation, ability to communicate at a high level, intelligence, ability to think both logically and creatively, overall demeanour and presentation. Their reputation, education and associations all add to their personal power in a negotiation. Perhaps the most important is their negotiating skills! The combination of some or all of these factors can far outweigh positional power, the value of which can disappear very quickly if gaps are exposed.

Although personal power is very real in the attributes, it is mainly perceived – that is people will see that you have those attributes because you display them, and they will then confer the power on you. If you should be bluffing, and they call your bluff, they will no longer view you as having personal power. They can't do that with the other two powers.

Personal power tends to be permanent – it is generated from within. Negotiators consistently work to increase their personal power, which includes their negotiating knowledge and skills.

The power of information. The expression 'information is power' is totally applicable to negotiation. The preparation stage is built around sourcing and analysing information to increase the power of the negotiator during the face-to-face meeting. No negotiator is happy with winging it. Even dealing with close friends or internal colleagues requires that you research your case before you negotiate with them. Buying a car privately? Guaranteed you've searched the papers for the last two weeks, made a list of the model and year you are looking at, the mileage and general condition, and then gone round the used car dealerships. And then the car fairs on the weekend. You take that negotiation very seriously, and part of your power will be the information you have gathered before you buy.

There is another aspect about information, which relates to all three power sources, that negotiators must be very aware of. 'Information is judged, for value or otherwise, against the source of that information.' Would you value advice about an investment provided by a failed business person? Probably not. What about your neighbour who runs a successful plant nursery, or your family doctor? Maybe. You'd probably say it would depend on what the investment was and how much they knew about it and whether they had relevant experience. What about the senior partner of the most respected fund manager? You'd probably say yes. And in a negotiation the other party must value the information that you contribute, so you need to portray yourself as the best source of the information. If you appear to be a reliable source of important and relevant information, your advice and guidance will be sought and valued. That is power. That helps you manage and control the negotiation process.

The power gradient ... how to manage when it's stacked against you

The power gradient refers to the way power is distributed between the parties in a negotiation. If you are running up a hill, the steeper it gets, the harder you have to work. If it's downhill you don't have to work so hard, and you may be able to coast. Negotiation is no different.

If one party has higher overall power, be it from one or all three sources, the result is invariably stacked in their favour. How do you effectively negotiate with someone who has a higher position than you in a large and prestigious organisation, has a greater range of decision-making authority than you have, and is regarded as an expert on the subject of your negotiation? With difficulty is the flippant answer! And yet we occasionally find ourselves in this position.

How do you think teenagers cope when they are up against powerful people, such as parents, teachers or police? The odds are heavily stacked against them – and they have to rely solely on their developing personal power. That's why they argue and sulk and fight and rebel. They have found the power gradient too steep to cope with.

Boss–staff negotiations are really no different. The boss has position power heavily in their favour. Decision power may be more balanced, as the staff member may have resources, such as technical ability, which are needed. They can also resign if they wish. That leaves personal power, and usually the boss will have a greater amount. Thus the staff member feels the power gradient working against them, and may revert to childish or habitual behaviour in an effort to redress the balance.

How negotiators can even the gradient

Position power. As it is real, there is very little you can do about this. (A supervisor can't become the equivalent of their manager!) However, if you are frequently involved in negotiations with people of higher status, consider the effect of a change of title.

I know of one businessman who negotiates business contracts for his company overseas every year. He has two business cards. The first states President & Chief Executive

Officer, and is printed on quality card. This gets him into any peer CEO's office, and works in his favour in negotiations. His other card is of lower quality, with the 'grand' title of Deputy Assistant to the Vice-President. This gets him into the lower levels of organisations, where he can freely chat to the people doing the things that his company is interested in. Deception? Yes, but probably harmless enough if he doesn't compromise his business integrity. (You decide on that one!)

One of the most respected and influential people I know in the rural industry refers to himself, even at the highest level meetings, as 'just a simple farmer'. You can imagine the information people are willing to share with him! An alternative way to redress the imbalance is to ask a more senior colleague, with greater power, to accompany you. Make sure your own position is not downgraded in the eyes of the other party.

Decision power. This is relatively simple to increase, provided, of course, you have the knowledge and judgement that goes with an increase. You can ask for discretionary authority over specific issues and variables, which enables you to work within a range (obviously your settlement outcome objectives range is the most appropriate). Or you can ask for limited authority, which above a certain point must be referred to someone else. This may apply to specific variables or the whole package, and can be very useful if you need an 'out' at any time. The main point with decision power is that if you are going into a negotiation with less authority than you need to agree the deal, perhaps you're not the right person to be there. Alternatively, take someone with you who has the necessary authority. Again, make sure your own authority is not downgraded; this can usually be covered by introducing your colleague as an expert in a particular area. You involve your lawyer or accountant in business negotiations, and provided the reason for having them there is appropriate, they are accepted.

> What counts is not necessarily the size of the dog in the fight – it's the size of the fight in the dog. **Dwight D. Eisenhower**

Personal power. This you can work on, and there is no limit. Negotiators who find themselves with position and decision power gradients against them work to increase their personal power. A former boss of mine, a director of a major multinational and chief executive of a large subsidiary, found himself in a negotiation with an 18-year-old, fresh out of college, working in a specialist technical field that he was professionally associated with, and studying for a degree part-time. His initial reaction, in his mind, was to write her off – but within minutes he realised that this person, young as she was, could transform a major part of the business. The youngster's personal power was so well based in the key areas that they got the deal and she went on to become a major contributor to the organisation.

When you are involved in preparing for a negotiation, you must consider the likely power gradient. That is why the background planning form includes details of the people involved, their position and their style of negotiation. You can then ensure your power sources and levels are sufficient to meet theirs. In negotiation, and indeed in most transactions between people involving relationships, the ideal power gradient should be slightly in your favour. Overuse or heavy use of any power should be avoided, as it may cause the other party to become defensive and reduce their willingness to cooperate or work towards a collaborative win/win.

For those readers who have childish power plays used against them – such as low seating, being kept waiting, telephone and people interruptions – my only advice is to keep your cool! Consider the consequences of any precipitous action you may like to take before taking it. You may win the battle but lose the war! Be assertive, adopt a professional manner, demonstrate personal power. This may well include asking for another chair, leaving and proposing another time, asking that calls be held.

Finally – remember the power of emotion (covered in Chapter 5) – the ability to give emotional satisfaction to the other party may well outweigh for them a material loss.

19 | Negotiating on price

The majority of business negotiations involve aspects of price as trading variables. And many general transactions have a component of price as an issue, for example contra-deals with internal customers in an organisation. So we have devoted a chapter to the topic of negotiating on price. Let's be very clear, however, that negotiations based solely on components of price (say, unit price, volume rates, discounts, rebates, bonus payments, payment dates, credits, etc) are less likely to achieve an expanded outcome; and where only price and discounts are involved, it will end up more a haggle than a negotiation! So bear in mind that we are discussing only one aspect within a total negotiation situation.

Where does price sit on the scale of relative importance in most situations? Fifth, behind function (will it do the job?); alternatives (is it the best for the job?); value (cost over time); back-up (service/support). Then the price.

That may not always be the case, but beware that you and the other party do not overrate price in your considerations.

Price is an emotional issue to most of us – even if it is not our own money! Our bottom lines are so often measured solely in monetary terms that we tend to focus on it. That is why your settlement outcome objectives form is so useful – it puts price in perspective. It's a bit like winning the battle but losing the war if we latch on to price issues at the expense of everything else.

During the discussion stage, resist any temptation or invitation by the other party to discuss price in detail. Repeat like a broken record:

'Yes, I have the issue of discounts on my list and am very

happy to discuss it in the context of value (or other variable).'

'Yes, I agree we appear to be more expensive than your imported materials, and I've noted on my list the need to discuss that fully. Let's get the other matters we need to discuss on the list as well, then we can look at the whole package together.'

'Yes, your volume does warrant a special deal, and it's on my list for discussion. Let's . . .'

During the expansion stage, you must be totally clear and fully informed about the pricing policy of your company and the industry. You cannot fudge your responses on pricing – your statements and decisions must be unequivocal. Any hesitation on your part may be taken as a sign of weakness and the issue will be forced by the other party. When exploring pricing issues, keep the whole package in mind, and constantly link it in with other items such as service, guarantees, technical support, added value, quality, etc.

During the trading stage, use the trading tips covered in Chapter 15 – they will ensure your overall bottom line is protected.

Finally, if you are a little slow with the calculator, don't be rushed during trading. You always hear of the case where the decimal point was left out. Don't let it be you! Always look at your figures for reasonableness. Your settlement outcome objectives form is your guide here. If you are not confident with a calculator, don't use it. Stick to your favourite method – it may take a little longer but you will stay within your comfort zone and not panic!

Price and cost . . . be clear on the difference

Price is not the same as cost. Although most people recognise this, they still tend to talk about them as if they were.

Price is what you pay to obtain ownership of the product or service or whatever you are negotiating.

Cost is what your outlay is over the period you own the product or service or whatever.

The price of phone/fax unit A is $750 and that of unit B is $950. If the machines performed the same functions, used the same paper, processed faxes at the same time and rate, the annual service cost the same, and they both needed replacing after three years, you would say that the price of A was less than that of B.

If, however, the cost of servicing A was higher than that of B, and it needed replacing after two years, you would say that A had a lesser price than B but cost more.

The distinction is important. It is the lifetime cost that you must negotiate on. If in the phone/fax example you were negotiating on price only, then A would get the business every time. It is only when you bring cost into the equation that you see the true lifetime cost.

That does not mean that cheaper items are inferior. Far from it. There are many products and services that are available across a wide range of prices, and price is as much a function of design, country of origin, exchange rates and demand as it is of quality. And why would you need to buy a commercial water-blaster when a domestic-sized, moderate quality one is perfectly adequate for home use, and will last a lifetime?

As a negotiator, therefore, separate your price requirements from cost considerations. Examine both factors separately, and then combined, to establish the true lifetime cost.

'Only when everything else is equal does price become the determining factor.'

With FMCG (fast-moving consumer goods) and similar high-volume/low-margin products, your pricing policies and expectations are more competitive and volatile. Lifetime cost does not apply in the same way, though factors such as branding, point-of-sale material, merchandising support, demonstrations, specials, advertising support and subsidies, incentives, etc, are all part of the price/cost issues, and must be presented and considered as a package.

Value . . . only when they know

'Perception is reality' – a statement bandied about. What does it mean in relation to price, cost and value?

If people see a price, or are quoted a price, then that price is real – there is nothing else for them to relate it to. It is separated from cost, and gives very little indication of relative value. So if you advertise a price of $10,000 on your vehicle, (car for sale – $10,000, phone . . .) but give no other relevant details, it is virtually impossible for anyone to assess its value, and certainly not its cost!

Value is made up of three things: the price of the product or service; the benefits that the product will provide; and either what the competition are offering or the opportunity cost (what else you could buy with the money outlaid). Until the buyer knows those three aspects, they cannot accurately assess value.

'Value only exists in the mind of the person (or buyer) who knows' – the onus is on the party presenting the product or service to demonstrate value.

As a negotiator, you must know price, cost, benefits and competitive pricing in order to adequately cover pricing issues and variables. A lot to absorb, but it sure beats ignorance!

Benefits . . . not just facts

In Chapters 7 and 8 we discussed variables in detail. We clarified that variables were aspects that could be traded, whereas fixed aspects were not. Whether fixed or variable, each one is made up of facts (features, what is built into the aspect) and benefits (what it will do, what the person gets out of it).

Let's take an aspect that applies to a whole range of negotiations – time of delivery. The family negotiation over a curfew, or the amount of car usage, has a time of delivery factor. The buying and selling of a boat has a time of delivery factor. An employment contract has a time of delivery factor. And the purchase of a mainframe computer has several points of time of delivery.

- The factor or aspect or issue is time of delivery
- The variables of time could be urgent, overnight, next week, midnight, standard, same day, sub-60, international, shipped, air-freight, air parcel, DX, confirmation, tracking, etc.

Each sub-variable has facts and benefits. Which is more important to the party you are negotiating with? Obviously what it does or will do is more important than what you call it, or how you manage it internally. If they are negotiating to improve the speed of delivery throughout their branch network, they want to know that your overnight (time) delivery service will mean their parcels will be picked up every night from their depot, and by 10 the next morning will be delivered to each of their 20 branches. Now that is a benefit. They do not need to know that you employ 35 drivers in Toyota vans from four till midnight, and another lot from midnight till 10! Vital to you, but of little real interest to them!

As a negotiator, you have the responsibility of separating facts from benefits, and emphasising those benefits that will match the other party's needs. Negotiation usually includes finding solutions for problems or maximising opportunities, and identifying and 'selling' benefits is a legitimate role of the negotiator.

Price wars . . . the road to haggling

In the introduction to this chapter, we stressed that negotiations based solely on price were really haggles. That may seem an unjustified distinction to those of you who spend most of your negotiations locked in price discussions with your respective suppliers or customers. You put just as much knowledge and skill into your negotiations as those who have a broad range of variables to trade with, and that's true.

Your responsibility, then, becomes how best to minimise the effect of competitive pricing, to raise the awareness of the other party to all the other benefits of buying from or selling to you, and achieve the highest level of sales or purchases at the best margins for your organisation.

To do that you need all those attributes listed under personal power in Chapter 18, and the specialist knowledge of your particular industry, such as FMCG touched on above. 'Knowledge is power' is totally applicable to your situation. And look very hard at all the scenarios suggested during your 'what if' sessions.

Discounts . . . stop!

Discounts come straight off the bottom line. Unless discounts are built into the cost of sales, or overheads, their effect is devastating. A simple example, Figure 35, shows the effect of a 'small' discount on the net profit of an average company.

Figure 35: Effect of discount on profit

	No discount		'Small' discount
Our sale at 'list' price is	$100		$100
We give a discount of	nil	of 3%	3
We receive net	100		97
Our cost of sales are	64		64
Our gross profit is	36		33
Our overheads are	28		28
Our net profit before tax is	8		5

Our 'small' discount of 'only' 3% has resulted in a huge 37.5% reduction in our net profit! Note: These figures are typical across most industries.

When discretions are high – and used indiscriminately – the result is more devastating, as Figure 36 demonstrates.

Figure 36: Effect of high discount

		No discount	'High' discount
Our sale at list		$100	$100
Discount of 10%		nil	10
Net revenue		100	90
Cost of sales	64		
Overheads	28	92	92
Net profit		8	(2)

Indiscriminate discounting can lead to bankruptcy! Discounts may be used if they generate sufficient extra volume to achieve the desired profit (see Figures 37 and 39).

When discounts are linked to sales revenue in a negotiation, the situation is manageable, as Figure 37 illustrates.

Figure 37: Discount generating extra sales

		Sales without discount		Sales with discount
Sales		100		150
Discount		Nil		15
Net revenue		100		135
Cost of sales	64%		64%=96	
Overheads	28%	92	28	124
Net profit before tax		8		11

Negotiating on price

Profit up 37.5%. Note that overheads do not increase like cost of sales; however with significant and sustained higher sales they would inevitably increase, and profit would reduce – possibly below the profit from sales without discount!

And when negotiation actively manages cost of sales and overheads, a significant boost is given to the bottom line, as in Figure 38.

Figure 38: Effect on profit by reducing costs through negotiation

	Existing situation		**Negotiation reducing costs**
Sales	100		100
Cost of sales	64	(3%)	62
Gross profit	36		38
Overheads	28	(7%)	26
Net profit before tax	8		12

By reducing costs of sales (materials, labour, freight, etc) by 3%, and overheads by 7%, the net profit has been boosted by 50%!

Given these effects, skilled negotiators learn to resist giving discounts and search for other ways to provide value to the other party. In terms of trading on costs and values, a discount is one of the highest swaps you will have, so you must maximise the return you get for every percentage point you trade.

For those of you who are buyers or sellers, Figure 39 shows the number of sales that have to be made to make up for a discount given at selected gross margins. Thoughtful reading!

Figure 39: Effect of discount on sales volume

Before You Cut Your Price STOP. Check this handy table to see how many more units you have to sell to get the same dollars. Find the percentage increase in unit sales you will need to equal the gross profit at regular price.

	\multicolumn{8}{c}{If your present gross profit is:}
	5%	10%	15%	20%	25%	30%	40%
If you cut your price	\multicolumn{7}{c}{You need to increase sales by ____% to achieve the same profit}
1%	25.0%	11.1%	7.1%	5.3%	4.2%	3.4%	2.5%
2%	66.7%	25.0%	15.4%	11.1%	8.7%	7.1%	5.3%
3%	150.0%	42.9%	25.0%	17.6%	13.6%	11.1%	8.1%
4%	–	66.7%	36.4%	25.0%	19.0%	15.4%	11.1%
5%	–	100.0%	50.0%	33.3%	25.0%	20.0%	14.3%
6%	–	150.0%	66.7%	42.9%	31.6%	25.0%	17.6%
7%	–	233.3%	87.5%	53.2%	38.9%	30.4%	21.2%
8%	–	–	114.3%	66.7%	47.1%	36.4%	25.0%
9%	–	–	150.0%	81.8%	56.3%	42.9%	29.0%
10%	–	–	200.0%	100.0%	66.7%	50.0%	33.3%
11%	–	–	275.0%	122.2%	78.6%	57.9%	37.9%
12%	–	–	400.0%	150.0%	92.3%	66.7%	42.9%
13%	–	–	–	185.7%	108.3%	76.5%	48.1%
14%	–	–	–	233.3%	127.3%	87.5%	53.8%
15%	–	–	–	300.0%	150.0%	100.0%	60.0%
16%	–	–	–	400.0%	177.8%	114.3%	66.7%
17%	–	–	–	566.7%	212.5%	130.8%	73.9%
18%	–	–	–	–	257.1%	150.0%	81.8%
19%	–	–	–	–	316.7%	172.7%	90.5%
20%	–	–	–	–	400.0%	200.0%	100.0%
21%	–	–	–	–	525.0%	233.3%	110.5%
22%	–	–	–	–	733.3%	275.0%	122.2%
23%	–	–	–	–	–	328.6%	135.5%
24%	–	–	–	–	–	400.0%	150.0%
25%	–	–	–	–	–	500.0%	165.7%

EXAMPLE: If your present gross margin is 20% and you cut your selling price 5%, locate 5% in the left-hand column. Now follow across to the column headed 20%. You will need to sell 33.3% MORE units to earn the same gross profit as at the previous price.

$$\frac{\% \text{ price cut} \times 100}{\% \text{ gross margin minus } \% \text{ of price cut}} \quad \begin{array}{l} \% \text{ needed} \\ = \text{sales unit increase} \end{array}$$

NOTE: Gross profit is defined here as gross margin × volume. This table holds gross profit constant by increasing volume proportionally with incremental decreases in gross margins. It should be remembered that this table refers only to gross profit and not to net profit which is: (gross margin − per unit costs) × volume.

20 | Building trust and credibility

Trust . . . you have to earn it
Suspicion is to be expected in any negotiation situation. The very act of suggesting that something may need to be 'negotiated', as distinct from discussed or talked through, may raise immediate apprehension.

Ricardo Semler, Brazilian business guru and author of *Maverick*, said that when they introduced flexitime, the suspicion was so high that the union asked: 'What's the catch?' When told: 'There isn't any,' they refused to believe it. They hunted through the company employment policies, and finally found something – workers were allowed to be up to five minutes late each day. 'Ha!' they exclaimed, 'you're trying to cheat us of 25 minutes each week.'

Trust in people is the ability to be able to rely on them and have confidence that everything they say and do will be true, worthy and reliable. When you are negotiating with people for the first time, this confidence is not possible. Although their reputation may be impeccable, you will need to experience it yourself before you personally believe it. Reversing the situation, you cannot expect people who meet you for the first time to trust you either!

The organisation you represent will add weight to your reputation, and most companies jealously guard and resolutely protect their reputation – whether it be their brand, their ethics, their values, or their fairness in negotiation. When negotiating within the business environment, therefore, you can take some comfort when you know the value system of the party you are dealing with. Negotiators must uphold their companies'

> Don't compromise yourself. You are all you've got. **Janis Joplin**

reputations to support others in the organisation and future dealings.

So how do you earn the trust of others, whether as a parent, a partner, a neighbour or friend, a business colleague or the negotiator across the table?

- Be professional in representing your organisation to its standards and values
- Be professional in meeting the expectations of the other party in terms of your behaviour
- Demonstrate an appropriate level of knowledge about their organisation and their situation
- Manage, or contribute to the management of, the negotiation process in a skilled and controlled way
- Demonstrate that you have appropriate levels of power
- Follow up the negotiation as agreed
- Ensure that you and your organisation fulfil all actions agreed in the negotiation
- Keep all personal promises or commitments
- Be ethical in terms of both organisations' value systems
- Respect diversity
- Focus on interests and problems, not personalities or positions

Those criteria apply to any level or type of negotiation. A child has unconditional trust in the parent, and if it is ever betrayed it kills the love. If you abuse the trust of a friend, you lose them for ever. If you betray the trust vested in you by your organisation, you will be fired. And if you do not keep the promises you made in a negotiation, they won't do business with you again!

It's not what you say . . . but how you look and say it

We spend a considerable amount of time preparing the words we are going to say, and in a negotiation there will be certain parts where you are, in effect, on show and making a presentation. It is important that in these instances the words are carefully thought through before being spoken. Examples are:

- Greeting – names and positions must be correct
- Opening gambit – the words you use are very important
- Conditional close on the shopping list – it should be word perfect
- Use of open questions to probe assumptions should be prepared
- Use of proposal phrases – 'What if . . . then perhaps . . .'
- Rules for brainstorming – the exact rules
- Problem-solving process – the sequence of events

When trading, remember:
'What if . . . then . . .'
'You will . . . then I will . . .'

Despite the importance of the words we use, however, they account for only 7% of believability. The most well-publicised research in this area was conducted by Professor Albert Mehrabian of the University of California. His research showed that believability and credibility, which are the basis of building trust, came from three factors:

- 7% Verbal: the words used
- 38% Vocal: the tone, or intonations – the way we say them
- 55% Visual: gestures, or body language – how we look when we say them

The expression 'it's not what you say but how you say it' sums this research up pretty well!

What does this tell us?

- First impressions do matter – it takes about 10 seconds for lasting first impressions to be made
- Our own belief in our statements will be picked up subconsciously by the other party

> You never get a second chance to make a first impression. **Anonymous**

- Our tone of voice will convey what we really think about them, their proposal, etc
- Our body language will reinforce what we are saying; it will be congruent
- Our body language will support our truthfulness, sincerity, concern, etc
- The actual words we use, though important at critical times, are far less significant than we may think for establishing trust and credibility

Presentation . . . are you believable?

Would you believe this person?

We all hold perceptions of what people in certain positions or situations should look like in terms of their personal presentation. You don't wear a suit to negotiate with your neighbour. You wouldn't normally be unshaven and unkempt when negotiating with the boss. Try conducting a complex business negotiation when you're in bright casuals and they're all in dark suits, and you're likely to be politely asked by your team negotiators to get dressed!

You set your own rules, of course, but for business negotiations the best attire is slightly more conservative than the industry standard.

Ethics . . . values in action

Your personal values must mesh with your organisation's values. If they are out of synch, they will create contradictory and inconsistent messages for the other party. This will affect the negotiation itself, and the implementation of the outcome agreed. Long-term relationships are very difficult to sustain when value systems are at variance.

If you are regularly involved in negotiations on behalf of your business or company, develop a set of guidelines to follow in terms of principles and values. It could contain short statements on the following:
- External customer service
- Pricing
- Quality assurance
- Contracts and documentation

- Authorities and delegation
- Prudential requirements
- Team negotiations
- Recourse procedures
- Financial regulations

> To be persuasive, we must be believable.
> To be believable, we must be credible.
> To be credible, we must be truthful.
> **Edward R. Murrow**

21 | Communicating with power

Inform . . . and confirm
Open for information – closed for confirmation! The golden rule for questioning. What does that mean? Remember Rudyard Kipling's verse: 'I kept six honest serving men, they taught me all I knew. Their names are What and Why and When and How and Where and Who.' When you start a question with any of these words, you are seeking information. The youngster who badgers you with: 'Why?' The colleague who asks: 'What do you want in that report?' The boss who quizzes you with: 'And who are you going to involve in that decision?'

You can't answer any of those with a one-word reply – at least not reasonably! A few words of explanation are required to satisfy the questioner; some thought has to be given to the response. If you answer the youngster with 'because', they'll keep on badgering! And if you short-change your colleague or the boss (the home or office one), you will find they become more persistent and demanding in their questions.

We somehow feel obliged to answer questions, and when they're open ones we tend to give fuller answers. Closed ones tend to get short answers. I vividly remember a radio interviewer questioning a coach about the performance of her team. 'Are you happy with their performance this season?' 'Yes,' was the reply. 'Will you be changing the line-up for the next test?' 'No,' was the response. 'Will they be fit for the test, bearing in mind the injury level?' 'Yes.' I cringed as I listened. Ask her an open question, you dummy, I mouthed! 'Do you think the selectors have anything to worry about?' I held my breath – but it still didn't draw out more than 'Not really'. He gave up, hung up, and with an exasperated tone said, 'Whew, that was like getting blood out of a stone!' I almost phoned him up and abused him for a gross example of inept questioning, especially from someone who should know better. Closed questions are for confirmation, not information. So use them as they were intended.

As a negotiator, you need to be a skilled questioner. At times you will want information, so make your questions open. And when you want to probe something, ask another open question.

Let's say you're in the discussion stage of the negotiation, and you want to know how important the settlement date is to the other party.

Start with: 'Why do you want settlement at that time?'

Then follow with: 'How would you feel about two weeks later?'

Or: 'What would be the effect of me wanting an earlier settlement?'

You'll get full answers – and be informed!

But there are points throughout the negotiation when all you want is confirmation, or a decision. So don't ask an open question; make it closed.

'Is settlement on the 31st OK?'

'Will you buy the timber if I get the paint?'

'We agreed on the amount – are you happy with the deal?'

'Did you hear me? Curfew's at midnight!'

When you're preparing for a negotiation, you should think about the information and decisions you want. We suggest you prepare some of those questions in advance – thinking about them formally often highlights other items and may even change the way you approach a particular issue. But please don't have a list of 20 prepared questions and ask them one by one – communication is between two intelligent beings, not robots! Ask sufficient questions to get the information you require to achieve the objectives of the negotiation. If you are working towards a win/win the other party will not mind answering reasonable questions.

But that does beg the question of you answering questions! Let's spend a few minutes examining this.

You don't have to answer questions . . . if you choose not to.

You do have a choice! You can choose whether you will answer a question or not, and you can choose how you will answer it. Now, I am not suggesting that you act like some politicians, who are notorious for evading the issues raised by questioners; they provide partial and often misleading replies and are adept at changing the question to suit their own agenda. (You know the one: 'Now if you had asked me my views on the timing of that policy, I would have answered . . .' and they proceed to answer their own question!) But they do offer us negotiators some insights into the way we respond to questions. Information is a vital ingredient in negotiation, often a source of power, and the consequences of giving information must be carefully considered. This does not negate the principle of win/win – in fact, information used wisely can enhance outcomes, and certainly creates a more favourable emotional climate. If you give information away freely, what value does the other party place upon it? If it is confidential to you, what does giving it away do to your credibility? If it is essential to your bottom line and you let it slip, what chance is there of achieving your settlement objectives – and thus a win/win? No, without doubt you must think carefully before responding to questions. What can you realistically do?

- Answer part of the question. This can be done with integrity: 'I can give you the information on the quality issue, but the specification aspect is not my area.' Or: 'The last part of your question I can answer, but the first part is confidential.'
- Turn it into a specific question that you can answer: 'You're asking me about the price of the materials. If we can turn that into the cost of the materials, I can tell you, because there is an important difference between the price and the cost.'
- Return the question to the questioner: 'You're asking me about the price of the materials. What do you think would be reasonable, given the quality we're talking about?'
- And if you want to play the politician, answer another question – yours! 'Now I'm pleased you asked me that, because that raises the other important issue of the rental. I think that should be linked to commercial rates because of

the location.' And then you could even add: 'Wouldn't you agree?'

The key to answering questions is: Put brain into gear before opening mouth!

> Talking is sharing, but listening is caring.
> **Zig Ziglar**

From ignoring . . . to empathic

I've always been fascinated about how we humans listen – or to be more accurate, not listen! In my wife's family there are three sisters, plus mother. They have developed, through many years of practice, a skill of listening to four simultaneous conversations about totally different topics, and are able to recall, in considerable detail, the matters and accompanying feelings and thoughts of the other three. I don't know how they do it – but as I said they do practise! But most of us don't practise, and we are not taught 'listening' at school, not even as a life-skill! And yet we spend over half our waking life listening. As negotiators we must be good listeners – our settlement objectives rely on getting the right information, and getting it right! How?

In simple terms, by being attentive to the other person. And what does that mean in practice? Well, there are a number of Don't rules. I prefer Do rules, and the main ones for negotiators are:

- Do focus on what they are saying, and their tone
- Do remain objective about the person
- Do listen for the meaning behind the words
- Do give them our undivided attention
- Do take notes
- Do avoid distractions
- Do control our emotions
- Do wait until they have finished speaking before preparing our response
- Do keep the roaming mind in check
- Do keep an open mind about the issue

- Do ask them to repeat something we missed
- Do let them have their say without interrupting
- Do use encouraging body language
- Do make positive verbal responses
- Do play back their ideas

If we practise these 'Do's', we'll be well on our way to being empathic listeners. We need to get beyond the selective stage!

Quality/level of listening (y-axis)

Empathic (Listens and interprets facts, information and feelings. Recognises what is 'not said'.)

Attentive (Listens and interprets facts and information. Focused mind and body. Good eye contact.)

Selective (Tunes in and out. Listens only to items of interest. Partial attention.)

Pretending (Not listening. Mind on self or elsewhere. Body language appears attentive.)

Ignoring (Not listening. Mind elsewhere.)

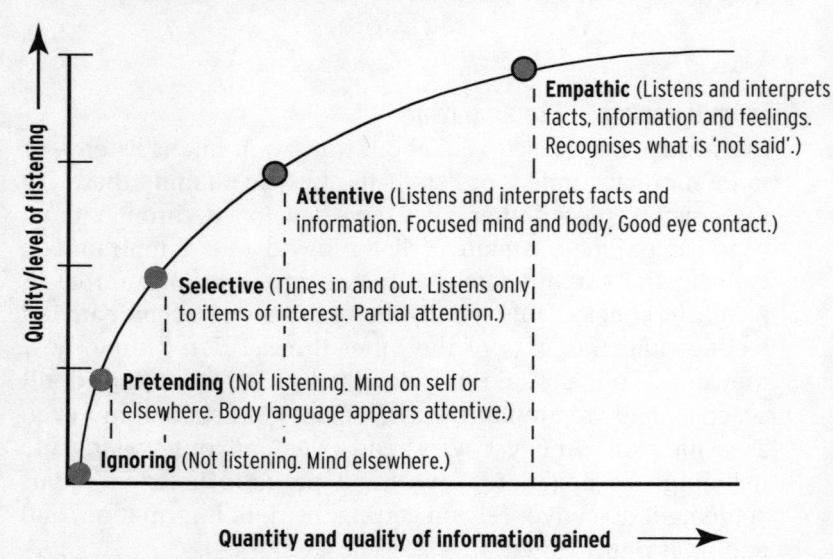

Quantity and quality of information gained →

Figure 40: Levels of listening

> We have two ears and only one tongue in order that we may hear more and speak less.
> **Diogenes**

Fact or fallacy ... the persuasive power of argument

I well remember my feelings of utter dismay when I opened the textbook for Philosophy 1. It was entitled *Logic*. For a right-brainer, this was anathema! I quickly re-enrolled in Political Science 1 – a much more amenable topic for a 20-year-old economics student!

Yet looking back, that topic – logic – would have been an

invaluable business tool. And for most negotiations, the ability to argue with logic, and refute illogical forms of argument, is an essential skill. And the use of argument forms is not limited to business – teenagers are pretty skilled at adapting 'logic' to their own advantage! When our position is challenged, we defend it. The other party will try to defeat our argument. Whether they know they are using faulty logic or not is irrelevant – what is important is our recognition of the fallacy and ability to point it out.

Here are some commonly used tricks of argument:

Generalisation: The delivery schedule you're proposing won't do. Your previous shipments have been late.

Quoting an irrelevant authority: This planned alteration to the packaging machine is bound to cause problems to the night shift. My neighbour is an airline pilot and he says it won't work.

Conforming: All our other suppliers do it. So should you.

Misuse of statistics: Eighty per cent of my age group are flatting. (Survey showed eighty per cent of those students at university were in student flats.)

Illogical form: All products we import are made from steel. Some steel products are powder coated. Your product is made from steel, therefore it should be powder coated.

Appeal to everyone: Everyone knows that big companies make huge profits.

Reasonable thinking: Any reasonable buyer would accept that condition. If you're not willing to agree to it you are being unreasonable.

Composition: Rates of pay are set annually. Performance reviews are conducted annually. Therefore rates of pay are always related to performance reviews.

The part and the whole: This figure quoted for the door frame is $10 too high. The whole house alteration quote must be wrong.

Splitting the difference: The fairest thing to do would be to split the difference.

Using jargon to impress: We've specified in the FJ470 unit as the GJ170 is underspecified for your analysts.

Pretending to not understand, supported by prestige: I've been a project manager for twenty-five years and I've never heard of a Gantt chart being used that way.

Appeal to emotions: Oh, come on. No loving parent would turn that request down.

So look out for these when you are negotiating, and remember age has nothing to do with their use!

> Anyone who thinks he knows all the answers isn't up to date on the questions.
> **Frank Lawrence**

22 | What negotiations do you find yourself in?

Relatives

For those of us with relatives – be they children of any age, parents, brothers or sisters, grandparents, and in-laws by any means – we know the added complications that blood brings to a negotiation. Blood relationships can bring baggage from the distant past, high emotions, split loyalties, 'bad blood' and a future link that is hard to sever. But they can also bring high trust, lifelong commitment, forgiveness, mutual care and support, and a long, satisfying partnership.

When we are negotiating with children we have a responsibility to see that their interests are fully met. Adults have considerable power over children, despite the child's ability to say *No*! A win/win role model throughout the early years establishes in the child an abundance mentality, an assertive mode of behaviour, and a balanced and realistic approach to managing transactions.

Teenagers pose different problems for adults; logic and assertion seem to be powerless to deal with the occasional irrational and emotional outbursts! Thankfully it does pass, and teenagers respect the adult who persists in conducting negotiations with them in a win/win manner.

The process of win/win works perfectly for relatives, children and teenagers, with some added cautions:
- Prepare as if it was a first meeting – don't assume too much
- Consider a BATNA, for them as well as yourself
- Allow them to save face

- Keep an open stance – no 'hidden agendas'
- Opening gambits should be focused on a win/win
- Use notes, charts and diagrams to convey points
- Remain positive – behaviour breeds behaviour
- Choose the location thoughtfully – whose ground is best?
- Stay calm if pressured – family emotions run higher than usual
- Accommodate unusual approaches – remain flexible
- Have sound reasons for your non-negotiables
- If needed – settle for slightly less materially
- Be generous with giving emotional satisfaction
- Really listen to what is not said – absorb facts and feelings
- Write up the final agreement – it avoids misunderstandings later

Business partners and close colleagues

In many ways these relationships are not dissimilar to negotiating with relatives. Many of us spend more time with our working partners and colleagues than we do with our real families. So the above comments apply equally, with some additions.

- A single lie destroys a whole reputation for integrity (Baltasar Gracian). Don't!
- Do not presume on the basis of friendship
- Keep business negotiations at arm's length
- Do not confuse *friend* with *friendly*
- Avoid obligations, past or future
- Do not place yourself, or them, in a compromising situation
- Adopt the Fair Go rule – could you defend your actions on TV?
- Familiarity breeds contempt – keep the negotiating process formal

Other negotiation relationships

It is not possible to cover the myriad negotiation types or situations in a single, readable book. There are specific texts available in written and internet form covering specialist negotiations like hostage, industrial, trade, diplomatic, political, etc. And then there are negotiations involving gender issues, remote locations, written only, teams, etc. Contact our **Negotiation Help Line** (refer page 222) if you cannot locate information you need; we will endeavour to source or recommend a source.

To help you develop your own negotiations we have prepared some checklists for some common negotiation situations. We have included a mind-map for the first three. They may give you a head start in preparing your variables and other issues, or at least stimulate the grey cells!

HOUSE SALE

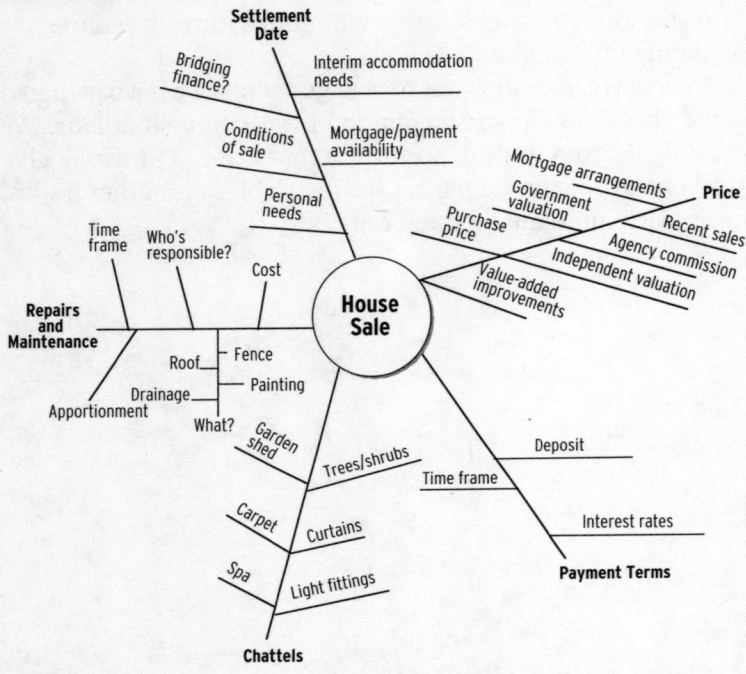

Mind map branches from central "House Sale" node:

- **Settlement Date**: Bridging finance?, Interim accommodation needs, Conditions of sale, Mortgage/payment availability, Personal needs
- **Price**: Mortgage arrangements, Government valuation, Recent sales, Purchase price, Agency commission, Independent valuation, Value-added improvements
- **Repairs and Maintenance**: Time frame, Who's responsible?, Cost, Roof, Fence, Drainage, Painting, Apportionment, What?
- **Chattels**: Garden shed, Trees/shrubs, Carpet, Curtains, Spa, Light fittings
- **Payment Terms**: Deposit, Time frame, Interest rates

Price
- ☐ Agency commission
- ☐ Mortgage arrangements
- ☐ Recent sales in the area
- ☐ Government valuation
- ☐ Independent valuation
- ☐ Purchase price
- ☐ Value-added improvement

Settlement Date
- ☐ Interim accommodation needs
- ☐ Bridging finance
- ☐ Mortgage availability
- ☐ Conditions of sale
- ☐ Personal needs

Repairs and Maintenance
- ☐ Who's responsible?
- ☐ Cost
- ☐ What? (e.g. roof, painting, drainage, etc)
- ☐ Time frame
- ☐ Apportionment of cost

Payment Terms
- ☐ Deposit
- ☐ Time frame
- ☐ Interest rates

Chattels
- ☐ Spa
- ☐ Trees/shrubs
- ☐ Light fittings
- ☐ Garden shed
- ☐ Curtains
- ☐ Carpet

REMUNERATION PACKAGE

Remuneration Package (mind map)

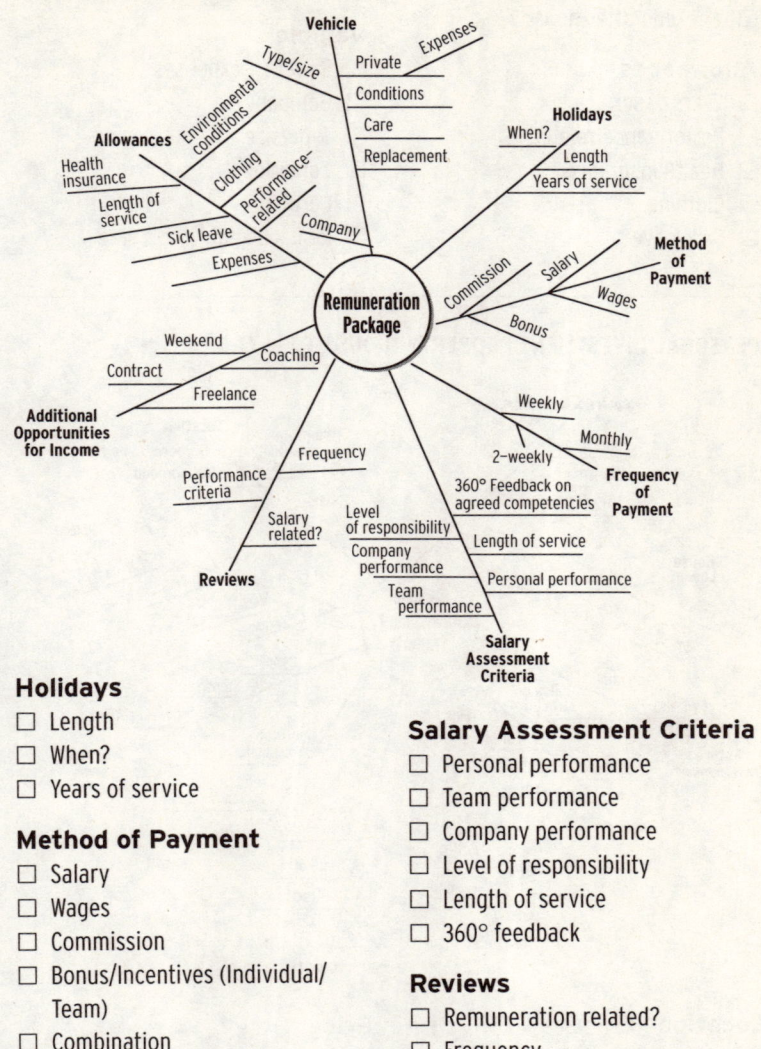

- **Vehicle**: Type/size, Private, Expenses, Conditions, Care, Replacement
- **Allowances**: Environmental conditions, Clothing, Performance-related, Health insurance, Length of service, Sick leave, Expenses, Company
- **Holidays**: When?, Length, Years of service
- **Method of Payment**: Commission, Salary, Wages, Bonus
- **Frequency of Payment**: Weekly, 2-weekly, Monthly
- **Salary Assessment Criteria**: 360° Feedback on agreed competencies, Level of responsibility, Company performance, Team performance, Length of service, Personal performance
- **Reviews**: Frequency, Performance criteria, Salary related?
- **Additional Opportunities for Income**: Weekend, Contract, Coaching, Freelance

Holidays
☐ Length
☐ When?
☐ Years of service

Method of Payment
☐ Salary
☐ Wages
☐ Commission
☐ Bonus/Incentives (Individual/Team)
☐ Combination

Frequency of Payment
☐ Weekly
☐ 2-weekly
☐ Monthly

Salary Assessment Criteria
☐ Personal performance
☐ Team performance
☐ Company performance
☐ Level of responsibility
☐ Length of service
☐ 360° feedback

Reviews
☐ Remuneration related?
☐ Frequency
☐ Performance criteria

Additional Opportunities for Income
☐ Freelance

What negotiations do you find yourself in?

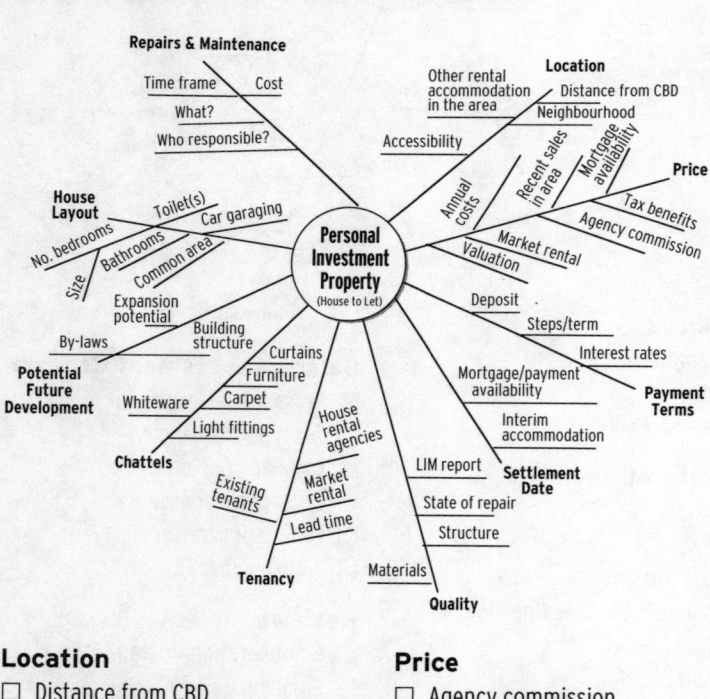

- ☐ Contract
- ☐ Coaching
- ☐ Weekend/after-hours

Allowances
- ☐ Years of service
- ☐ Performance-related
- ☐ Health insurance
- ☐ Clothing
- ☐ Sick leave
- ☐ Environmental conditions
- ☐ Expenses

Vehicle
- ☐ Private – expenses
- ☐ Company
- ☐ Type/size
- ☐ Conditions
- ☐ Care
- ☐ Replacement time-frame

PERSONAL INVESTMENT PROPERTY (HOUSE TO LET)

Mind map centred on "Personal Investment Property (House to Let)" with branches:

- **Repairs & Maintenance**: Time frame, Cost, What?, Who responsible?
- **Location**: Distance from CBD, Neighbourhood, Accessibility, Other rental accommodation in the area
- **Price**: Tax benefits, Agency commission, Mortgage availability, Recent sales in area, Market rental, Valuation, Annual costs
- **Payment Terms**: Deposit, Steps/term, Interest rates, Mortgage/payment availability
- **Settlement Date**: Interim accommodation, LIM report
- **Quality**: State of repair, Structure, Materials
- **Tenancy**: Existing tenants, Market rental, Lead time, House rental agencies
- **Chattels**: Curtains, Furniture, Carpet, Whiteware, Light fittings
- **Potential Future Development**: By-laws, Building structure, Expansion potential
- **House Layout**: No. bedrooms, Size, Bathrooms, Toilet(s), Common area, Car garaging

Location
- ☐ Distance from CBD
- ☐ Accessibility
- ☐ Neighbourhood
- ☐ Other rental accommodation in the area

Price
- ☐ Agency commission
- ☐ Tax benefits
- ☐ Mortgage availability
- ☐ Recent sales in area
- ☐ Valuation
- ☐ Market rental

- [ ] Annual costs

Payment Terms
- [ ] Deposit
- [ ] Term
- [ ] Interest rates

Settlement Date
- [ ] Interim accommodation
- [ ] Mortgage/payment availability

Quality
- [ ] Structure
- [ ] Materials
- [ ] State of repair
- [ ] LIM report

Repairs and Maintenance
- [ ] Time frame
- [ ] What?
- [ ] Who's responsible?
- [ ] Cost

Tenancy
- [ ] Existing tenants

- [ ] Lead time
- [ ] Market rental
- [ ] House rental agencies

Chattels
- [ ] Curtains
- [ ] Light fittings
- [ ] Carpet
- [ ] Furniture
- [ ] Whiteware

Future Development Potential
- [ ] By-laws
- [ ] Expansion potential
- [ ] Building structure

House Layout
- [ ] Car garaging
- [ ] Bedrooms (no./size)
- [ ] Common area
- [ ] Bathroom(s)
- [ ] Toilet(s)

FAMILY HOLIDAY

Location Options
- [ ] Attraction needs
- [ ] Interests
- [ ] Distance
- [ ] Travel costs
- [ ] Accommodation (alternatives/cost)

Research
- [ ] What information?
- [ ] Who's responsible?
- [ ] Time frame

Pets
- [ ] How accommodated (out/in)

Who's Coming?
- [ ] Family
- [ ] Friends

Bookings
- [ ] Travel
- [ ] Accommodation
- [ ] Other
- [ ] Costs
- [ ] Who's responsible?

Time Frame
- [ ] Desirable
- [ ] Application for leave
- [ ] Costs

Resources
- [ ] Travel
- [ ] Accommodation
- [ ] Boat/Equipment
- [ ] Other

Budget
- [ ] Costs
- [ ] Funding
- [ ] Who's responsible?
- [ ] Time frame

TEENAGER STAYING-OVER AT FRIENDS FOLLOWING PARTY

Time Frame
- [ ] Drop off at 'stay-over' home
- [ ] Pick-up from 'stay-over' home
- [ ] Pick-up from party

'Stay-over' Parents
- [ ] Pick-up time from party
- [ ] Drop-off
- [ ] Pick-up
- [ ] Form of transport
- [ ] Bedding/clothing/food needs
- [ ] Contingency plan (contact phone no.)

Conduct Assurances
- [ ] Party controls
- [ ] Attitudes (level of coop./openness)

Security
- [ ] Phone numbers
- [ ] Driver(s)
- [ ] Friends
- [ ] Contingencies

Transport
- [ ] Parent(s)
- [ ] Friends
- [ ] Public
- [ ] Other

Costs
- [ ] Total costs
- [ ] Source of revenue

Dress
- [ ] Party
- [ ] Stay-over home

Who with?
- [ ] What friends?
- [ ] Party – communicate with organisers (those responsible)

BIRTHDAY PARTY

When?
- [ ] Appropriateness/convenience
- [ ] What occasion?
- [ ] Who decides (consultation)?

Venue
- [ ] Location
- [ ] Accessibility
- [ ] Size
- [ ] Availability
- [ ] Who decides (consultation)?
- [ ] Parking

Invitations
- [ ] Who to invite (consultation)?
- [ ] Who to organise?
- [ ] Invitations (printing/distribution)
- [ ] Responses
- [ ] Time frame

Resources
- [ ] Food
- [ ] Music
- [ ] Drinks
- [ ] Decorations
- [ ] Who's responsible?
- [ ] Time frame

Controls
- [ ] Inform neighbours
- [ ] Drink/drive
- [ ] Door surveillance
- [ ] Costs
- [ ] Budget
- [ ] Who manages budget?
- [ ] Who meets costs?

IN-HOUSE COMPUTER UP-GRADE

Problems (with current system)
- [ ] Capacity
- [ ] Capability
- [ ] Congruence (re current and future needs)
- [ ] Downtime (speed, mistake)
- [ ] Costs (running, failures, maintenance, etc)
- [ ] Presentation

Delivery
- [ ] Time
- [ ] Costs (and who's responsible)

Price
- [ ] Budget
- [ ] Terms
- [ ] Resale value (depreciation)
- [ ] Trade
- [ ] Size/volume

Installation
- [ ] Conditions
- [ ] Flexibility
- [ ] Downtime
- [ ] When?
- [ ] Who?

Benefits
- ☐ Capacity
- ☐ Expected lifespan
- ☐ Flexibility
- ☐ Servicing
- ☐ Cost savings

Training
- ☐ Needs
- ☐ Cost

- ☐ Who (pays)?
- ☐ Who (facilitates)?

Servicing
- ☐ Costs
- ☐ Who's responsible?
- ☐ Response time
- ☐ Costs

COMMERCIAL LEASE

Maintenance
- ☐ Lift
- ☐ Airconditioning
- ☐ Flooring
- ☐ Response time
- ☐ Common areas
- ☐ Who's responsible?

Cleaning
- ☐ Offices
- ☐ Windows (in and outside)
- ☐ Common areas
- ☐ Costs
- ☐ Who's responsible?

Signage
- ☐ Rights
- ☐ Size
- ☐ Positioning

Service Areas
- ☐ Toilets
- ☐ Kitchens
- ☐ Waiting areas

- ☐ Access
- ☐ Who's responsible?

Parking
- ☐ How apportioned
- ☐ Maintenance
- ☐ Usage rules
- ☐ Access

Alterations
- ☐ Constraints
- ☐ Costs
- ☐ Who's responsible?

Lease
- ☐ Interest rates
- ☐ Reviews
- ☐ Assessment criteria
- ☐ Sub-tenancies

PRODUCTION TEAM LOWERING REJECT RATES

Failure Costs (of present situation)
- [ ] Reject rates
- [ ] Costs of rework
- [ ] Costs of material waste
- [ ] Morale of team
- [ ] Impact on customers

Suppliers
- [ ] Involvement (who to liaise?)
- [ ] Impact of supplier quality

Incentives
- [ ] Incentives
- [ ] Team performance bonuses
- [ ] Involvement
- [ ] Motivation

Additional Resources
- [ ] Measuring processes and tools
- [ ] Plant
- [ ] Labour

Review All Processes
- [ ] Apply problem-solving tools and processes
- [ ] Measure
- [ ] Project team

Training
- [ ] Quality tools
- [ ] Skills and knowledge
- [ ] Teamwork
- [ ] New process
- [ ] Who's responsible?

Empowerment
- [ ] Responsibility
- [ ] Enablement
- [ ] Leadership styles
- [ ] Followership styles

Measuring
- [ ] What to assess
- [ ] Training

NEW SUPERMARKET PROJECT MANAGEMENT

Time Frame
- [ ] Target date
- [ ] Critical path

Planning Approvals
- [ ] Research
- [ ] Who's responsible?
- [ ] Time frame

Design and Planning
- [ ] Specifications
- [ ] Consultation and agreement

Costs
- [ ] Budget
- [ ] Consultation
- [ ] Monitoring
- [ ] Reviews (+ progress)

Financial Package
- [ ] Plan
- [ ] Consult
- [ ] Research
- [ ] Liaise financial institutions

Controls
- [ ] Agreed assessment criteria
- [ ] Measurement tools
- [ ] Monitor progress
- [ ] Contracts
- [ ] Communication process

Review Progress
- [ ] Analyse data
- [ ] Corrective action
- [ ] Involve all relevant parties

Tenancy
- [ ] Who's to facilitate?
- [ ] Complementary tenants (criteria)
- [ ] Application process
- [ ] Selection
- [ ] Contracts

Marketing
- [ ] Attract investors / tenants
- [ ] Who's responsible?
- [ ] Advertising (promotion)
- [ ] Opening (including organising)

MARKETING CAMPAIGN – ADVERTISING AGENCY

Objective
- [ ] Target market
- [ ] Level of penetration
- [ ] How to measure

Time frame
- [ ] Time frame
- [ ] Opening - why?
- [ ] Finish (of campaign)
- [ ] Critical path
- [ ] Realistic

Costs
- [ ] Critical path steps (what to include)
- [ ] Budget
- [ ] Breakdown
- [ ] Review
- [ ] Shared (and how apportioned)

Design
- [ ] Budget
- [ ] Brief
- [ ] Review
- [ ] Agreement

Review Progress
- [ ] Assessment criteria
- [ ] Who's responsible?
- [ ] Costs
- [ ] Contingencies

Advertising Medium(s)
- [ ] Budget
- [ ] Cost breakdowns
- [ ] Target market (how to reach)

In conclusion . . .

As a reader of fact and fiction I do appreciate a good ending. I can put a book down with a sense of closure, of understanding the boundaries, the feeling of somehow knowing what it was all about and therefore feeling comfortable and satisfied. These are the books that I talk about. If it's a business book I buy copies for my colleagues; I put post-it notes in my own and I highlight. If it does the rounds at the office, it's followed up vigorously as any number of my colleagues will want to steal it.

If it's non-business it will do the rounds of the family, and yes we talk about it, and even visitors are likely to get a memorable passage read over coffee whether they wish it or not!

These are the good books with the good endings. So when Bernice Beachman at Penguin had finished reading the text and phoned and said, 'It's good, but it needs an ending,' I knew exactly what she meant. But how to draw together a book about negotiation? A summary would be boring, and there are summaries at the end of each chapter. More self analysis? No – if the reader had worked through all the You Try It exercises that would be superfluous at this point.

And then I thought of all the people that I have met over the years who have talked to me about their negotiating successes and failures, and how they worked at improving their skills, and I realised what the ending should be. It should be based on those time honoured words: 'Success is a journey not a destination – half the fun is getting there.' The interesting thing about all these people was the fact that they were having fun and succeeding! Their recipe for success was simple – they tried it out. They went to the seminars, they read the books, they talked to the experts; they observed their colleagues and they tried it out.

They had long given up thinking 'If only I had done that when I asked for a raise,' or 'I only wish I had thought of that before we agreed.' When I recalled their individual recipes for success, there was a common theme:

- They believed they could do better
- They bought books, and went to lectures
- They asked their boss to come along and critique them
- They roped their colleagues in to come with them
- They insisted on being professionally trained
- They got their personal partners to act as a sounding board
- At work they debriefed, in detail, and put up with the ragging
- At home they went over what they did – point by laborious point
- Some of them admitted to getting lazy on the preparation, and falling back!
- But the majority said they got steadily better, and more confident
- Practically all said it had improved their relationships at home and work

So much for the journey – sounds tough! But not one person regretted working at it, and they recounted their failures with as much relish as their successes!

Have they found the journey worth it? Given that the majority of these people hold senior positions in corporations, or are owners or major partners in their own businesses, and are successful and happy with it, I guess they have. They have obviously done some very good deals. They may have made a few people unhappy on the way, but their philosophy is certainly abundance and win/win. Their relationships are wide and stable. People enjoy working for them and with them. Many are business mentors. They are confident in their abilities and comfortable with themselves.

They've had good fun on the journey achieving success at various stopping places on the way to their destination!

My recommendation?

Start now. With the very next negotiation, no matter how simple. Read this book in sections – say a chapter every weekend. Use a highlighter on the points that will help you improve. Swing your approach closer to a win/win, and practise being assertive. See if you can get a partner or colleague to work with you – it's always easier with someone else. Take the initiative in your next business negotiation, whether internal or external. Control the process, you'll be surprised how positively the other party responds. Over the next few weeks complete the You Try It exercises at the end of the chapters, and read the comments accompanying the answers in the Appendix. They include a number of helpful hints. Finally, don't give up! There is a lovely quote of Lloyd James:

Those who try to do something and fail are infinitely better off than those who try to do nothing and succeed.

And while you are trying, reflect on this:

Negotiation is the only game where two can play and both can win!

So start your play.

Appendix

Chapter 1
Aggressive: 1, 3, 6, 10
Passive: 4, 8
Assertive: 2, 5, 7, 9

Chapter 2
Step 1 – Define the problem.

Sue modified her wheels. She has no time to remodify. The dealer will have few buyers if not remodified. Both have the same objective – a quick remodification.

Step 2 – State cause/effect of problem.

We know the cause. The real problem is one of getting the remodification done quickly.

Step 3 – Generate ideas.

Sue could take time off work; persuade a friend to do it; find a wheel specialist who could do it quickly; renegotiate the trade-in price; ask the dealer to arrange on her behalf; ask the dealer to arrange on his behalf.

The dealer could renegotiate the trade-in price and have his mechanics do it; arrange to have it done but Sue pays; leave Sue to organise as best she can.

Step 4 – Evaluate ideas.

Sue discounts the first two and renegotiating. The dealer wants to keep her happy and so rejects his last idea.

Step 5 – Decide solution.

Both agree it is feasible for the dealer to find a wheel specialist to do the remodification at Sue's expense. The dealer has a mechanic who could do it during the lunch breaks. They select this last option on the basis that Sue will pay the mechanic for the hours worked.

Step 6 – Implement solution.

Sue signs a work order. Sue will bring the original gear in tomorrow. The dealer organises the mechanic's schedule.

Yes, this was a simple problem, but then most problems are when a process is applied to find a solution!

Chapter 3
This is a simple broad view of preparation for a negotiation. A more detailed checklist is included at the end of Chapter 10.

Comments on each behaviour:
1   A useful behaviour in most

situations. Two points to watch. Do not exclude others in the team, as each may have influence unknown to you. Singular focus can put undue pressure on the main person and antagonise the others.

2. For most of us this is the easiest approach. We know our own situation so well we can brainstorm a comprehensive list easily which will stimulate our thinking when we consider their needs. Purists may suggest looking at their situation first is more objective. You can achieve this by involving others in 'what if' sessions.

3. An excellent guide though take into account changed circumstances and current values.

4. A must for win/win negotiators. Use at all stages of a negotiation, not just preparation.

5. However much we dislike internal politics they exert considerable influence on the people and the positions taken on each variable. We must take them into account.

6. As long as you check out their approach in the early part of the discussion stage it is useful to assume they will be flexible. Your preparation for a win/win outcome will be more creative. Obviously if past experience suggests they may take other approaches you would factor this in.

7. Despite rapid change, personal relationships tend to be long standing, habitual and predictable. Business relationships are subject to influences beyond the control of individuals and may or may not match expectations.

8. Essential as it is a reasonable predictor of their attitude, approach and behaviour to this particular negotiation.

9. Emotional outcomes are often more important than the actual material achievements. By considering their feelings you may be able to achieve more material outcomes for yourself. Let them have the kudos – you take the cash!

10. Even for the mathematicians, all calculations are best written down. They also provide a visual proof if genuine calculation mistakes are made.

11. Important to prepare and contribute to your BATNA. Provides a degree of confidence.

12. A must. Particularly important to have a bottom line that you can live with.

13. Important to take account of feelings. This assessment may force you to review how you have valued and costed your variables.

14. Providing it does not compromise your position this consideration may provide emotional satisfaction for them.

15. Be prepared! Contingency planning applies to the people and their behaviours as well as the issues and variables involved.

16 In personal negotiations we tend to be more emotionally involved and a partner, friend or mentor is a worthwhile reality check. In business negotiations it is important that colleagues who may be affected by the outcome of your negotiation are consulted beforehand. Major companies have established think-tanks expressly for this purpose. 'What if' is their standard phrase!

17 The key is 'if it worked well'. We should always research their current situation and reassess their value system (teenagers' values are volatile and unpredictable) before we begin detailed preparation. Business negotiations are subject to changes in influences – both people and situational.

18 We often concentrate on the material aspects during planning, leaving the feelings until we are face to face. Best to include these factors from the start.

19 Having the basic paperwork prepared in advance is appropriate. A warning: if your paperwork is completed before you reach agreement the other party may resent your assumption, and take offence. This could result in a less than full commitment to this deal, or a reduced win/win approach next time.

20 This has to be the best assumption unless you are aware they will take another approach. Your preparation will still include contingency plans.

Scoring:
This checklist and scoring is based on broad general preparation behaviours adopted by successful negotiators. A more in-depth and specific checklist is included at the end of Chapter 10. The scoring is not based on scientific norms nor does it indicate the level of success. Negotiation outcomes are based on a range of skills, knowledge and judgement. Preparation is one of the inputs and influences. Your score indicates how well you prepare for a negotiation. The behaviours and the comments above apply to the most simple to the most complex negotiations – the depth and time taken will of course differ.

91–100 A consistent high level of preparation indicating a thorough understanding of key preparation factors and high application across all areas.

76–90 A high score indicating a wide application of preparation activities with a broad understanding. It will be relatively easy for you to work on those few areas where a marginal shift will mean you have total coverage.

61–75 You have several strong areas – so don't neglect them! Select two or three areas where you see improvement possible and work on those during your next preparation.

45–60 Review your 'seldom' and 'sometimes' areas. Select three or four which you believe you could easily work on and would make a significant difference to your confidence. Work on these in your next negotiations, no matter how simple the negotiation seems. Then review how you went, and the effect of your extra preparation on the outcomes.

Less than 45 may indicate several things. You may be new to negotiation, and these ideas are foreign to you. You may be aware of the need for preparation, but the opportunities to negotiate have seemed few and far between (though you will now realise that even the simplest of negotiations can benefit by thoughtful preparation). Or the low score may indicate a low level of understanding of the importance of preparation, or perhaps a lazy application! Whatever – select three or four areas which you know have let you down in past negotiations, and work on these when you next prepare. Best wishes!

Chapter 5

1 Let's explore why we have differing ideas about this holiday...
2 We need to consider why an allowance may be appropriate...
3 We should be able to work this out so that we are both comfortable...
4 We both have problems with this, but we need to reach an agreement...
5 We need to find a better way than either of us have come up with...
6 We need to make these changes but you must be happy to implement them...
7 Let's see if there are other options available to us...
8 The problem that confronts us both is time so let's work on that first...
9 Because our expectations differ markedly we need to discuss the reasons for our respective positions before we proceed...
10 There is a problem that we must confront. We need to find a way that solves the problem without affecting our relationship and is an acceptable solution for the teenagers...

Chapter 6

At first read this seems an impossible negotiation situation. Yet this is typical of most negotiations – each party has a different objective. So let's analyse and see if we can find some way around their seemingly divergent holiday dreams.

First let's agree their individual TFC for a holiday. I think we can say that Mother has a large gap – probably an 8. Father is more into networking than family, so his TFC might be slightly less – say 7. The teenagers definitely have a gap for any holiday – say 8.

Now we consider their TFC to holiday together. Mother would probably prefer to keep the family together, so hers would be an 8 or 9. Father wouldn't want to be seen taking another work holiday at traditional family time, so his would be an 8 or 9 also. The teenagers are going to be happy with or without their parents as long as they have suitable company, so their TFC for staying as a family may be as low as a 4.

Finally, let's consider their TFC to compromise. Mother is unlikely to compromise with Father as two young children on a boat for two weeks doesn't enthral her – say 3. She doesn't have to compromise with the teenagers as there is a surf beach and crowds of teenagers at the beach house, and they are happy with that if Colorado is a no-go. Father could probably persuade the teenagers that water skiing was OK though they are definitely not keen on sharing with young children – so their TFC to go with Father is a low 3. So Father is stuck with a family that has a TFC to go cruising of 3 – in other words an extremely unlikely event unless he can introduce some other variable that would change their values (like money – but we'll not develop that theme!)

Having done that quite straightforward analysis of their various tensions for change, we could develop a range of variables and associated benefits that would see a family holiday at the beach house, with a promise to Father that he would get preference next year!

Chapter 7

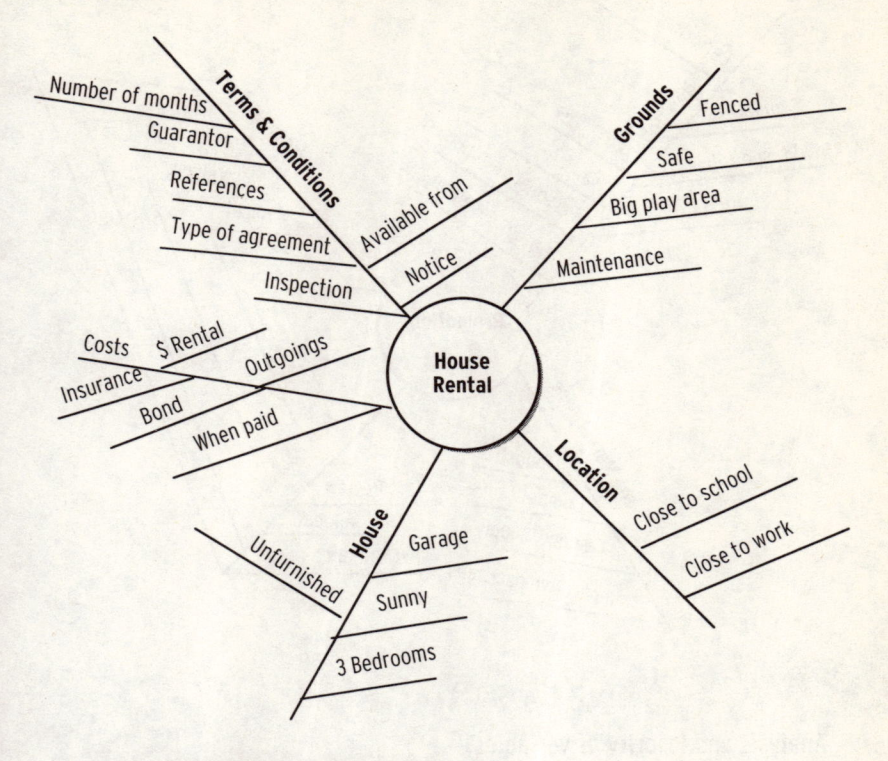

Mind map — House Rental:

- **Terms & Conditions**: Number of months, Guarantor, References, Type of agreement, Inspection, Available from, Notice
- **Grounds**: Fenced, Safe, Big play area, Maintenance
- **Outgoings**: Costs, $ Rental, Insurance, Bond, When paid
- **House**: Unfurnished, Garage, Sunny, 3 Bedrooms
- **Location**: Close to school, Close to work

Analysis and Priority of Variables

Essentials:
Maximum rent $300 pw
Term not less than 3 months
Term not greater than 12 months
1 month's notice
Return of bond
Landlord organises
   - repairs
   - maintenance

*Big play area
*Fenced
*3 bedrooms

Desirables:
Rent less than $250 pw
Landlord pays
   - outgoings
   - insurance
Landlord maintains
   - grounds
No guarantor

*Close to school
*Sunny

Non-essentials:
Payment dates
Inspection
Type of agreement
References

*Close to work
*Garage

* Fixed requirements. Not variable, but impact on decision

Mind map

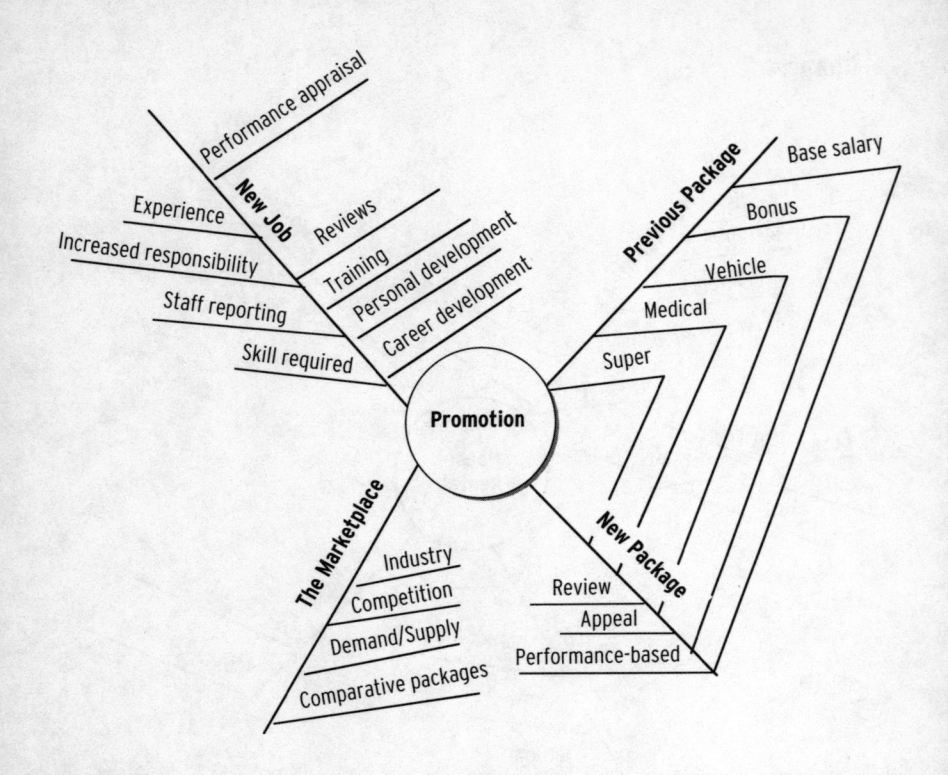

Promotion (central)

New Job:
- Performance appraisal
- Experience
- Reviews
- Increased responsibility
- Training
- Staff reporting
- Personal development
- Skill required
- Career development

Previous Package:
- Base salary
- Bonus
- Vehicle
- Medical
- Super

New Package:
- Review
- Appeal
- Performance-based

The Marketplace:
- Industry
- Competition
- Demand/Supply
- Comparative packages

Analysis and Priority of Variables

Essentials:
Base salary increase
  within 6 months
Super linked to base salary

Performance based
  bonus 3 months
Performance review
  in 3 months
Management training
  within 3 months

Desirables:
Base salary increase
  within 3 months
Vehicle upgrade
  within 6 months
Product training
  within 6 months
Personal development
  plan 6 months

Non-essentials:
Vehicle upgrade
  before planned
Career development
  plan
Appeal

* The Marketplace and New Job items used to 'sell' the variables

Chapter 8

	Aces	Swaps or Trades
High	Time of start Time of completion Service contract Pool cleaning contract Parent labour	Deposit Pupil supervision Discount on pool Progress payments Fencing contract Full landscaping contract Pupil labour Shed painting
Value to them (School)	**Fillers**	**No-no's**
Low		Contract – standard Truck and digger access Safety Water supply

Low — Cost to us (Poolside) — High

Note that to be able to rank the variable you must have control of the variable. This is always a gray area. Take the fencing contract. On the surface it is controlled by the School, and therefore Poolside would not 'own' it to rank. However in reality Poolside can strongly influence, even threaten, the School to give it the fencing contract. Thus it will be a 'swap' for both. Similarly the Service Contract is controlled by the School, but as Poolside are the only licensed contractors in the area, the School has little choice but to give the contract to Poolside. Control is often dual!

Chapter 9

1 Mind-map variables and issues

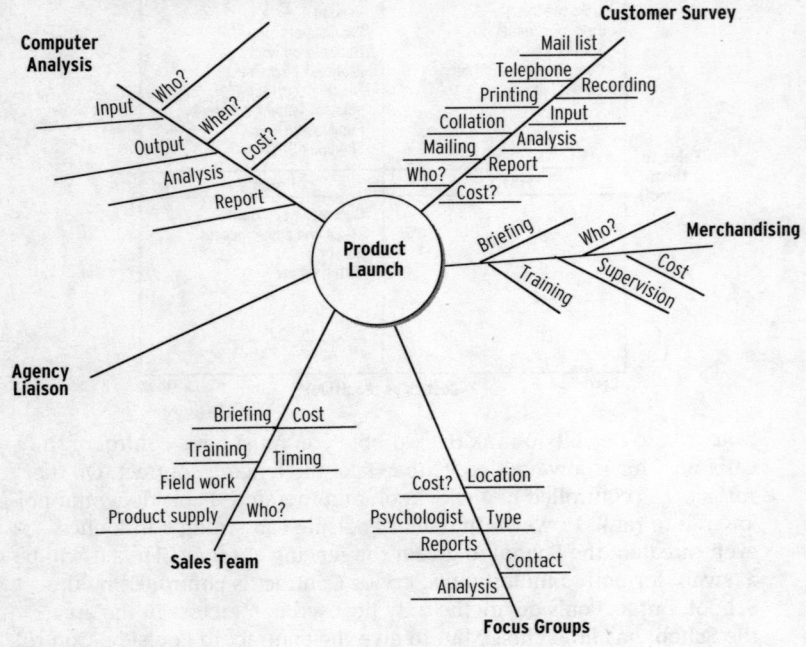

Computer Analysis: Input, Output, Analysis, Report, Who?, When?, Cost?

Customer Survey: Mail list, Telephone, Printing, Recording, Collation, Input, Mailing, Analysis, Report, Who?, Cost?

Merchandising: Briefing, Training, Who?, Cost, Supervision

Agency Liaison

Sales Team: Briefing, Cost, Training, Timing, Field work, Product supply, Who?

Focus Groups: Cost?, Location, Psychologist, Type, Reports, Contact, Analysis

Central node: **Product Launch**

2 Ranking

After prioritising all the items, and deciding what you were prepared to do, you were left with the following variables which you ranked:

	Aces	Swaps or Trades
High	• Supervise computer input/output for customer survey and focus groups • Brief the sales teams	• Run the focus groups • Prepare analysis and report for customer survey and focus groups • Supervise training of merchandisers • Fieldwork with sales teams
	Fillers	**No-no's**
	• Supervise printing and mailing of customer survey	• Product train sales teams • Brief focus group psychologist

Value to Product Manager (vertical axis: Low to High)

Cost to me (Sales Manager) (horizontal axis: Low to High)

3 Settlement Outcome Objectives

Variable	Priority	Value	Optimistic	Realistic	Pesimistic (bottom line)
Supervise Computer input/output – C.S. & F.G.	ESS	Ace	100%	85%	70%
			Reimbursement of Callum's salary		
Brief the Sales Team (by Sales Manager)	ESS	Ace	Travel & accommodation	50% travel subsidy	25% travel subsidy
Run the Focus Groups (2 x Sales Ho.)	DES	Swap	100%	90%	80%
			Reimbursement of Callum's salary		
Prepare Analysis & reports of C.S. & F.G.	DES	Swap	$10,000 fee	$7500 fee	$6000 fee
Supervise Training of merchandisers	ESS	Swap	100%	75%	50%
			Reimbursement of Kelly's salary		
Supervise printing & mailing of customer survey	NE	Filler	$800 fee	$600 fee	$500 fee
Fieldwork with Sales Teams	DES	Swap	Travel & accommodation	50% travel subsidy	25% travel subsidy

Chapter 10

1 A valuable practice. 'Weak ink better than strong memory' is a wise Chinese saying.
2 You need at least one creative method to capture all the ideas. If you prefer lists that's fine but do your initial capture on a mind map or similar. It is easier for others to contribute to a mind map.
3 It is easy to overlook a vital point. We become tunnel visioned. So use others.
4 Essential. If you don't you run the risk of cherry-picking, nibbling and escalation. You are also likely to pick up straw men and hidden agendas by preparing a full list. And a win/win outcome relies on a wide number of variables and aspects for expansion.
5 Prioritising is critical when we come to mapping out our settlement outcome objectives.
6 Empathy is both a skill and an attitude. You are well served if you have both.
7 Emotional satisfactions and outcomes are as important as material outcomes. If the other party feels that you have been fair and reasonable they will justify any material outcome they achieved.
8 Often the least well done. Every variable must have its own bottom line. Donation is avoided.
9 Why have an optimistic position if you are going to start from a lower one? You can go down but it is very hard to go up!

Appendix | 213

10 The golden rule for bargaining – trade on the basis of high value to them, low cost to me – these are the aces. Always value on the basis of: 'What is it worth to them?'
11 They are ideal for this, and can provide emotional satisfaction far beyond any material cost to you.
12 For all but the one-off deals working towards a win/win will achieve the best expanded outcome for both parties.
13 You can adjust the other party's style by being consistent with yours. Assuming that a win/win assertive style is the one you are adopting, you can counter an aggressive style by persisting with an assertive mode. Behaviour breeds behaviour. Become a student of body language.
14 Too many negotiators 'wing it' when it comes to openings, and they always regret not spending the few minutes thinking about setting the scene and gaining control. A chess player would not countenance such a lazy approach!
15 The most useful two words in the negotiation language. Don't restrict them to the preparation!
16 Knowing one's own tension for change helps in the accurate planning of positions and potential movements. It also highlights dangers if the TFC is high, and forces consideration of a BATNA.
17 Many negotiators only prepare one when their TFC is significantly higher than the other party's. But it can be prepared quite quickly and having one increases the confidence level which is important where there is an imbalance. Even in a family negotiation a BATNA should be preplanned.
18 Sometimes our negotiations have several fixed or non negotiable items. We must consider their worth and importance to the other party as if they were variables, and sell their advantages and benefits.
19 The ability to trade is the essence of negotiation and the more items that are available to trade the more creative and flexible you can be. However they must not be so split up that they become unmanageable – we need to be able to package them and link them with other variables. Also refer Chapter 15.
20 The time taken and the depth of preparation will obviously vary between negotiations, depending on complexity and our experience, but thoroughness will apply to all!

Scoring:
This checklist is a more specific inventory of your preparation behaviours than the first one in Chapter 4. The scoring is not based on scientific norms nor does it indicate the level of success. Your score does indicate how well you understand and

practise strategic and tactical preparation behaviours. There is a high correlation between full and correct preparation and achievement of outcome objectives.

91–100 Indicates a very high knowledge base with consistent application across all preparation activities.

76–90 Indicates a high level of understanding of preparation concepts with a consistently high level of application for most activities. Select one or two of your marginal behaviours and concentrate on them during your next preparations.

61–75 Some areas are well understood and applied – keep your application high on these strength areas. Review your weaker behaviours, and select two or three that you believe would make a significant difference for you. Bring these up to the same level as your current strengths. Once you have those mastered, work on another two or three.

45–60 You will have a few high scores based on aspects of preparation that you are comfortable with. Your challenge over the next few negotiations is to bring your low scoring behaviours up one or two points. It's really not too difficult if you are selective. Choose two or three to work on at a time. Spend a few extra minutes rereading and reflecting on that behaviour, and what you could do to improve the depth of application. When you finish each negotiation, go back over your preparation notes and decide which areas need some more work. It won't be long before you're scoring in the 80's!

Less than 45 If you are new to negotiation and just doing a quick read before you study this book in depth I would not be concerned. If you are involved in negotiations on a regular basis then I am worried – refer to the comments for this score at the end of Chapter 4 in this Appendix.

Chapter 11

1	Assertive	Win/win
2	Aggressive	Win/lose
3	Passive	Lose/win
4	Aggressive	Win/lose
5	Assertive	Win/win
6	Assertive	Win/win or win/lose
7	Passive	Lose/win
8	Assertive	Win/win
9	Assertive	Win/win or win/lose
10	Aggressive	Win/lose

Chapter 13

1 Yes. It appears they are deliberately delaying consideration of an item that should be dealt with now.
2 Yes. It appears they are isolating this item and want to get a firm decision on it now.
3 No.
4 Yes or No. Yes if they are trying for a quick decision before other items that might be linked are considered. No if it is an isolated item for both parties and they can make a tentative early agreement.

5. Yes. They appear to be saying that everything is on the list. What they intend to do is to add items after agreement on the current list is completed. A classic!
6. Yes or No. Same as 4.
7. Yes. 'Minor points' are never minor! And somehow by using a third party it doesn't sound as ominous.
8. Yes. Another classic! 'At the moment' means I'll drop it on you at the very end when you have nothing left to bargain with!
9. Yes and No. Yes if they are trying to keep a particular item off the agreed list. No if they are merely wanting to discuss the two items in conjunction.
10. Yes. Beware those who don't want a shopping list – they are cherrypickers par excellence!

Chapter 14

1. Expansion. This is a proposal.
2. Discussion. They are developing a combined shopping list.
3. Expansion. They're looking at alternatives.
4. Either. Discussion if they are wanting to avoid including the item on the shopping list. Expansion if they are proposing an item on the shopping list be covered in conjunction with another.
5. Discussion. Probably an attempt to cherrypick later.
6. Expansion. They are making a proposal with the expectation that both parties will consider ways to achieve it.
7. Discussion. Sounds like Dad's one-way list!
8. Either. Discussion if the child is adding their own item – an extra bonus – to the list. Expansion if the child is exploring ways to link extra pay for extra work; they have couched it as a proposal.
9. Expansion. Both creatively exploring alternatives.
10. Discussion. They are endeavouring to get all the relevant issues out and included on the shopping list.

Chapter 15

1. There are three issues here. The first relates to communication. If you instantly respond when they have finished speaking you are likely to appear arrogant; people like to feel that you have listened attentively and value their input. The second issue relates to perception of value. If you instantly respond to their offer in a positive way they will wonder whether they have offered too much. If you instantly responded negatively they will feel belittled. Either way you have failed to recognise their perceptions of value. The third issue is one of practicality. Any offer made during a negotiation demands thoughtful consideration. Most of us take a few seconds to think through the ramifications of even a simple offer. Major matters may involve time out. Message:

pause and think! You only have one chance to get it right.
2. Essential and based on the settlement outcome objectives.
3. Aces are the most valuable trading variables. Because they are low cost there is a temptation to give them away. That is why we always rank variables based on value to the other party.
4. Even the simplest of negotiations will have three or four variables and each variable three positions. And there are links between. So a written format is essential.
5. Taking an adjournment is always acceptable. (A caucus by definition involves a private meeting of your own group). It is OK to adjourn by yourself. After all we often talk about being in two minds about something! The key point is that you are prepared to say: 'I need to consider this in private.' Only warning – don't overdo.
6. You can't ask for a glass of water three times in an hour, and they might question your health if you request regular restroom breaks. Use a variety of methods.
7. You need to refer back and forward throughout the negotiations. Unless you have a mega memory you will not be able to recall the finer details of each proposal, option, decision or trade. 'Weak ink better than strong memory' as the Chinese saying goes.
8. Designed for encouraging movement, getting through an impasse, showing goodwill, useful ground bait.
9. Basic rule. Never make a decision if you feel pressured or out of your depth. Slow down or take a break. 'Decide in haste repent at leisure' is very relevant to negotiation. A caution: do not slow down to the point where the other party takes advantage of your slowness, or you begin to lose credibility.
10. Research consistently demonstrates that negotiators who maintain their optimistic settlement objectives throughout the negotiation achieve a higher level outcome. The point of settlement in a negotiation is based on belief as much as reality. Aim high is a mental attitude practised by winners in any field of endeavour.
11. Our body language sends more signals and information than the actual words we use. It doesn't mean we remain poker faced throughout but we must ensure the signals we send match our intentions.
12. Questions do not indicate doubt or weakness. You must be in total control of your responses at all times. Chapter 21 has some useful questioning tips for the negotiator.
13. The eventual agreement is made up of a number of individual agreements on a variety of variables. Variables

are traded individually, in pairs or linked. The settlement outcome objectives format allows you to see the relationship between the variables and the positions you can trade between. It is a package approach.

14 This is the mind set negotiators adopt. It is flexible and creative. It looks at each non-tradable item and asks 'what if' or 'why not'. There is usually some aspect of a constant which can be turned into a variable, or at least a benefit that can be 'sold'.

15 'Never make an offer without getting something in return' is a basic trading rule. If you do you lower the value of the concession you donate.

16 This gives greater ability to trade. Large movements indicate you have more to give and they may test this by asking for even more. The way you trade is sending signals – if you trade in small amounts they expect you to continue to trade in small amounts so will not ask for large movement. If you send signals that you are running out by incrementally reducing the amount you give they will believe you are getting close to your limit. Conversely if you signal your store is unlimited by giving out ever increasing amounts then expect ever increasing demands.

17 Make notes in your preparation if you think they will be included and check out during the discussion stage. Listen carefully as you get out their shopping list – you may detect straw men. Consider how you will deal with them.

18 Good! They should know that you are awake to their attempt and will not let them get away with it. They may not try it out in future negotiations if you firmly resist.

19 Why let them know how far you can go? They will push or lead you to your limit but not over. Authorities are precious – keep them private.

20 I hope you've answered 'almost always' or 'often'! Whether you love or hate bargaining it is stressful – how you treat it can be exhilarating or debilitating. The more skilled you are, the more prepared you are, the more confident you will be. You may eventually find the give and take of bargaining to be the most rewarding activity of the whole negotiation!

Scoring

This checklist and scoring is based on behaviours required to get the best possible deal during the bargaining stage of a negotiation. The scoring is not based on scientific norms nor does it indicate the level of success. Negotiation outcomes are based on a range of skills, knowledge and judgement. Bargaining is a crucial activity within the negotiation process but it depends heavily on how the negotiation has been handled up to that point. Your score indicates how well you manage the bargaining stage. The behaviours apply across all types and levels of negotiation. Only the range and complexity differ.

91–100 indicates a very high level of bargaining ability, underpinned by high knowledge and judgement. Your personal confidence is very high. You should be achieving most if not all of your optimistic settlement objectives and achieving a high level win in material terms. If you are inclined, you have the ability to develop a strong win/win in both material and emotional terms if you consider the other party's requirements throughout.

76–90 indicates a high level of bargaining skills and behaviours which should ensure you achieve most of your settlement outcome objectives at the realistic to optimistic range. As a slippage in one or two areas will work against you disproportionately I suggest you review each one 'often'. Compare these with your strong behaviours and see if you can make strong/weak links. You have the potential to achieve superior outcomes across your total range.

61–75 suggests there are certain behaviours that you are not adequately or consistently using. This will be disadvantaging you at this crucial stage. Select three or four of your weaker behaviours and work on these during your next bargaining. Review what happened and build on those areas which will have the biggest impact. Some of these behaviours are simple but do not neglect them on this count. Don't neglect your strong areas – keep those working for you. There is no reason why you cannot increase your bargaining ability significantly over a short period and make the best use of all your preparatory work.

45–60 indicates a number of areas which are limiting your bargaining ability. This may be limiting the size and the scope of the win/win you are achieving. Review each behaviour and how you have rated it. Which ones do you consider you could improve quickly with a small amount of effort? Which ones are OK now but if improved would add significantly to your confidence? Be tough on yourself – select five or six from these two lists and work hard on these during your next two or three negotiations. If you are able to review what happened with a partner, colleague or boss then do so. If by yourself then objectively review your actual performance against your objectives. Having an increased awareness of what is best practice bargaining behaviour is half the battle! You should be up in the high 80s in a short time.

Less than 45 may indicate several things. You may be new to negotiation and therefore many of the terms used foreign to you. You may be doing them but not to the extent required to be really successful. You may be doing a few to a high level but failing to achieve because there are so many gaps. Whatever the reason there is hope! Understanding underpins commitment, commitment underpins practice. Select those behaviours that you think will make a significant difference in your next negotiation. Read, think and plan. Then use them! Best wishes!

Chapter 16

1 'We agreed that the rate we were paying was more than adequate to cover any extra time needed. So if you want me to look at anything extra for the last day I'd need to reduce the hourly rate overall. Do you want me to do that?'
2 'It might make it easier for you but the loading configuration I've devised won't take it without some adjustment. If you want the extra on I can do it but it will cost you extra in handling fees.'
3 'If you want Mark to stay over I don't mind but it will mean that you have to clean out the rumpus room today instead of next week. I didn't think you had time for that?'
4 'No it's not I'm afraid. We had agreed that three o'clock was the deadline and I've scheduled it for a morning job out of town. If you really want it by ten you'd be in for a transfer fee. Is it that critical?'
5 'Unfortunately Friday evening's not suitable. If you can't get it back Thursday as we arranged, then you'll have to return it on Monday but you'll have to pay the weekend fee.'

About our Canadian group of companies

We operate throughout Canada, with business seminars run regularly in Calgary, Halifax, Moncton, Ottawa and Toronto. In-house programmes are conducted for clients around the world.

Negotiation programmes are provided on a pre-scheduled public basis at all five locations. In-house programmes are specifically designed and tailored to meet clients' needs in terms of level of staff, type and complexity of negotiations, organisation and industry requirements.

Other business training programmes include sales at all levels, sales management, key account management, marketing, customer satisfaction, presentation skills, performance management, project management, management, leadership, teams, coaching, attitudes and motivation, self management, influencing, tactical and strategic time management, strategic thinking and change management.

The seminars are led and tutored by a team of business-proven senior associates. Teams of locally based account managers advise clients on all training needs. Performance consulting is provided for in-house clients by the senior associates.

We can be contacted at:
Calgary: Phone (403) 233 7448 or Fax (403) 233-7173
Halifax: Phone (902) 443 5805 or Fax (902) 457 2475

Moncton: Phone (506) 857 4181 or Fax (506) 857 9733
Ottawa: Phone (613) 729 2111 or Fax (613) 729 7814
Toronto: Phone (905) 640 5515 or Fax (905) 640 5526

Negotiation Help Line:
e mail: plc.toronto@prioritymanagement.com

Index/Glossary

The explanations of the words and terms included in this Index/Glossary are not dictionary definitions, but in most cases they reflect common usage. I have explained them in the way that they are generally used in negotiations. The list is by no means exhaustive (for example there are numerous terms invented by practising and academic negotiators relating to bargaining tactics that are only used in certain types of negotiations). If I have missed your favourite term, you have two choices: contact me on the Help Line or refer to another book!

The first or main chapter reference is included.

above-the-line When the combined shopping list is agreed a line is drawn under the list. All items above are for subsequent discussion. Contrast with below-the-line. Ch.13

abundance A win/win approach that views the world and therefore the negotiation situation as having sufficient to go around – everyone can get what they want. Creative and expansive. Contrast scarcity. Ch.1

ace A variable which is of high value to the other party but costs you little. Use to advantage. Don't be tempted to give away. Ch.8

adjournment A break to enable private reflection or discussion, or to relieve pressure. Can be used at any time. Also called recess. Ch.17

agenda Set after introduction formalities. Covers

	time, logistics, procedures and order of discussion. Use to control the process, not to cover the content. Ch.13
aggressive	An attitude and behaviour that is dominant, often hostile and offensive. Essentially win/lose. Competitive verbal and non-verbal behaviours. Ch.1
agreement	Both parties confirm common understanding and decision on an issue, figures or details. Occurs throughout a negotiation. Final agreement includes all prior sub agreements. Ch.16
aim high	The attitude of being able to achieve the optimistic objectives set. The behaviours follow the attitude – positiveness, creativity, persistence, reinforcement, selling value, maintaining opening positions, etc. Ch.1
assertive	An attitude and behaviour that respects the rights of others whilst maintaining own rights. Confident and direct. Essentially win/win. Ch.1
assumption	Formed during preparation. Necessary to make but must be checked out for correctness. Ch.10
attitude	The mental approach to negotiation with resultant behaviours. Usually based on past and habitual. Colloquially win/win, win/lose, etc attitude. Ch.1
bargain	An alternate term for trade, exchange, give and take. Ch.15
BATNA	Best Alternative To a Negotiated Agreement. (From Roger Fisher and William Ury, *Getting to Yes*. Boston: Houghton-Mifflin, 1981). A contingency plan or option if no agreement is reached, or when it appears during the negotiation that an unacceptable loss will occur. Ch.6
behaviour	Verbal and non-verbal conduct usually

	based on current predominant attitude. Colloquially e.g. aggressive behaviour, competitive behaviour, win/lose behaviour. Ch.1
below-the-line	Any issue that is raised after the combined shopping list has been closed off. Leaves the option to disregard or reopen for discussion prior agreements. Refer cherry-picking. Contrast above-the-line. Ch.13
benefits	Items of worth which are fixed or non-negotiable. Need to be 'sold'. Ch.7
bluff	A tactic used to give the impression of power, position, strength, etc, which one does not have. Essentially a deceit with intent to mislead. Ch.17
body language	Signals, messages and information sent by conscious or subconscious non verbal bodily gestures or postures. Ch.20
born trader	Someone who is regarded as having been born with the instincts of a trader, 'a natural'. Ch.15
bottom line	The settlement position taken with every variable below which you will not go. Often called pessimistic position. Also refers to overall minimum outcome position. (Often breached by ill-prepared negotiators). Ch.9
bragging rights	Being able to talk or boast about the deal one got. Comes from emotional satisfaction and may not be based on material outcome. Ch.5
brainstorming	A creative process used to produce (from the mind) as many ideas as possible about a situation, issue, etc. Mainly used during preparation, but can be used during expansion stage or when problem-solving. Ch.2
broken record	The tactic of repeating a statement or

	message a number of times in order to wear the other party down into accepting it. Ch.19
bullying	A form of aggressive behaviour used by the strong against the weak to influence their behaviour. Occurs when there is a power imbalance. Also refer intimidation, threat. Ch.17
caucus	A break in discussions to allow a private meeting within a group. Used throughout a negotiation as a time strategy. Ch.17
cherry-picking	The tactic used to obtain a final agreement on one issue at a time. It enables one party to achieve what they want from each variable without the other party being able to link with other variables during subsequent trading (hence cherry-picked). Ch.13
close	Any action or statement that seeks to get a decision on an issue or final agreement. A term commonly used in selling. Equivalent to 'finalise' in negotiation. Ch.16
collaborative	An approach and behaviour which believes that by working with others rather than against them will achieve better outcomes. Essentially assertive and win/win. If overly collaborative could be lose/win. Contrast competitive. Ch.1
competitive	An approach and behaviour based on the belief that by being aggressive or opposing the other party one will achieve more of what one wants. Usually win/lose, but may be win for self only. Contrast collaborative. Ch.1
compromise	Giving something up. In negotiation this should always be two-way, and therefore considered an exchange rather than compromise.

concession	An item that can be traded or given. As it has some negative connotations the term variable is usually preferred.
conditional close	The question asked at the end of the process of developing a combined shopping list. Also any question obtaining a decision that is subject to a subsequent event. Ch.13
constant	An item that is not able to be changed in any way. Hence opposite to variable. May be fixed or non negotiable. Ch.7
contingency	An alternative course of action should the intended outcome appear unlikely. Considered during the preparation stage. Often done formally as a BATNA. Ch.6
cost	The amount that is paid over the lifetime of a product or service. Contrast price. Ch.19
credibility	Belief in a person (or organisation) based on their combined verbal, vocal and visual actions and behaviours. The level of credibility determines the amount of trust and believability we have of them. Ch.20
current reality	The situation as it exists right now. Contrast desired outcome. Ch.6
deadline	A tactic that puts a time for acceptance on the offer; usually in order to pressurise a decision on an unreasonable offer.
deadlock	The point where the parties cannot move forward on any issue. Sometimes called stalemate. Usually a restart or mediation needed. Compare impasse. Ch.17
deal-breaker	An issue that causes one or both parties to withdraw or threaten to withdraw from the negotiation. Ch.7
debriefing	A meeting following the negotiation to compare the actual outcome with the plan. Covers all issues including the

	behaviours and responses during the negotiation. Ch.16
desirables	Variables and other issues that you would like to have as part of the final deal, but which will not break the deal if not included. Contrast essentials and non-essentials. Compare like-to-haves. Ch.7
desired outcome	The position or situation you would like to be in at the end of the negotiation. The results you would like to achieve from the negotiation. Contrast current reality. Ch.6
discretionary authority	Authority given to a negotiator to vary the normal terms and conditions of one or more variables, within specified limits or range. Ch.15
donate	Give away a variable or item of value without getting anything in exchange. A negotiation sin! Contrast trade. Ch.15
done-down	A colloquial term for losing. Usually relates to a material loss. Also ripped-off, screwed. Ch.5
emotional outcome	The feelings held at the end of the negotiation. May relate to one or all factors including the people involved, behaviours, environment, time, material outcomes compared to plan, etc. Compare material outcome. Ch.5
empathy	The ability to 'sit at their side of the table'. Assisted by high level of questioning and listening skills and reading of non-verbal behaviour. Ch.21
entrenched	A fixed attitude or position taken by one party. If set for more than two or three issues, likely to be a competitive stance.
escalation	An attempt to gain an extra amount from a variable or a number of variables after final agreement has been confirmed by both parties. Compare nibbling. Ch.17
essentials	Those variables or items that must form

	part of the final deal. Also called must-haves. Contrast desirables, non-essentials. Ch.7
exchange	Term meaning swap, give and take, bargain, trade. Ch.8
face value	The perceived or apparent worth of a variable; in negotiation always check it out. Ch.8
fallacious argument	A form of argument based on false logic; used to persuade or justify own position, or defeat the other party's argument. Ch.21
filler	A category of variable which is low value to one party, low cost to the other. Used as public relations, a 'giveaway', groundbait, goodwill. Also see ace, swap, no-no. Ch.8
final offer	The final position taken by one party when trading a variable. A point of settlement if accepted. Often a bargaining stance used to test movement. Ch.15
finalise	The final stage in a negotiation when one or both parties initiate an end to trading and agree the final deal. Also involves recording the agreement and documentation. Ch.16
first impressions	The impact each party makes and receives on first meeting face to face. They last. Ch.13
fixed	A non-tradable item or position. Contrast variable. Ch.7
gap	Distance between a current situation and desired outcome for each party. Also the gap between the two parties' desired outcomes. Ch.6
gap analysis	A descriptive evaluation and estimation of the size and strength of the gap(s). Also tension for change analysis. Ch.6
give and take	Another term for swap, trade, exchange, bargain. Ch.15

giveaway — A variable of low value to one party and low cost to the other. Used to reinforce relationship. Refer filler. Ch.8

good-guy bad-guy — A tactic using two negotiators. The first negotiator is very unreasonable but is then replaced by the second who acts reasonably. The tactic is designed to encourage the other party to make quick decisions with the reasonable negotiator – to their disadvantage.

goodwill — Positive gesture by one party using a low cost variable which, despite being of low value to the other, indicates support. A filler. Ch.8

ground bait — A variable of low cost to one party and low value to the other, used to entice or attract interest in another variable or issue. A filler. Ch.8

haggle — A low form of bargaining, more aptly termed a wrangle or squabble. Usually occurs when few variables available to trade, with low creativity. Ch.19

hidden agenda — Undisclosed items, issues or positions. May indicate a competitive approach. Ch.17

hierarchy — The pecking order in a negotiation team or organisation. Gives position and decision power. Refer power, power gradient. Ch.18

impasse — A point reached where both parties are unable or unwilling to move on a variable or variables. Usually surmountable by changing tack, using another variable to create movement elsewhere, or employing problem-solving. Also refer deadlock. Ch.17

interests — The stake a party has in part or all of the negotiation, and the outcome. Often a personal position, involvement or

	investment. Usually involves emotion. Ch.4
intimidation	Behaviour by one party to influence the thinking and thus behaviour of the other party through fear (of consequences). Can be used by weak against strong (blackmail). Also bullying, threat. Ch.17
issue	Any matter or topic included in the negotiation. May be fixed or variable.
leverage	The influence a party holds over any issue or situation through power or authority. Also gearing in financial terms.
like-to-haves	Issues or variables which a party would prefer to be included in the outcomes, but are not essential to the deal. Also called desirables. Ch.7
limited authority	An authority level vested in or delegated to a negotiator for the purposes of this negotiation. May cover one or more variables, or the total deal. Compare discretionary authority. Ch.15
lose/lose	An outcome where although an agreement is reached neither party views it as satisfactory. May be a material or an emotional loss, or both. Ch.5
lose/win	An outcome where one party considers they have lost at the expense of the other (the winner). May be a material or emotional loss, or both. Ch.5
manipulation	A control or influencing behaviour to create an advantage. May be devious (probably competitive) or skilful to enhance a win/win outcome. Ch.12
material outcome	A result that is measured in absolute monetary or tangible terms. Contrast emotional outcome. Ch.5
mind-mapping	A creative technique (Buzan) to capture thoughts and feelings about any topic or issue. Refer creativity. Ch.2

minor point	Presumably a small issue, and although it may be it is often an expression used to conceal a major issue and should be treated with caution. Ch.13
movement	The shift between positions in the range of a variable during trading. Also progressive exchanges between each party. Ch. 15
must-haves	Issues or variables that a party considers integral to the negotiation and must be part of the outcome. Also called essentials. Contrast desirables, like-to-haves, non-essentials. Ch.7
neutral	An emotional control of thought and behaviour that keeps the view of the situation objective, and moving neither forwards or backwards.
nibbling	A tactic used to obtain a little bit more from one or more agreed outcomes, but before the total deal is finalised. Compare escalation. Ch.17
no deal	An outcome of the negotiation where both parties decide that no agreement will be reached. Ch.5
non-essentials	Issues or variables that if not included in the negotiation will not be deal-breakers. Contrast essentials, must-haves. Ch.7
non-negotiables	Variables ranked as non-negotiable because they are low value/high cost, and thus too costly to trade. Ch.8
non-verbal	Bodily behaviours commonly called body language that impart signals and messages. More important conveyors of meaning and believability than verbal behaviours. Ch.20
opening gambit	An opening action and/or statement that is intended to gain the initiative in the early stages. Ch.11
opportunity cost	The opportunity given up by choosing an

	alternative (to spend, to accept, etc). Ch.19
optimistic	An outcome position for a variable. The minimum level of opening when making a proposal on that variable. Also refers to the mental approach. Also refer realistic, pessimistic. Ch.9
outcome	The point of settlement for each variable. Also the final agreement in terms of win/win, etc. Ch.5
package	A combination of two or more issues or variables to more effectively trade. Ch.9
passive	A submissive mode of verbal and non-verbal behaviour. Allows others to invade (territory, boundary). Contrast assertive, aggressive. Ch.1
patronise	In the positive sense means to use, support or be a customer. In the negative sense it means to treat the other party in a condescending way.
perceived power	Power assumed held through position, status or behaviour. Not real, but may have same effect if perception is maintained. Ch.18
persuasion	The power of influencing. 'Might' or may not be 'right'. Ch.21
pessimistic	The bottom line settlement outcome objective for a variable. Contrast optimistic, realistic. Ch.9
point of settlement	Where agreement is reached on each variable. Also the overall agreed outcome. Ch.16
politics	The influences on a negotiation from internal power relationships. May be difficult to control.
position	The rank or status held in the hierarchy. Confers position or status power. Refer power and power gradient. Ch.18
power	The ability to control or influence the behaviour of others, by use of a power

Index/Glossary

	source. Refer power gradient. Ch.18
power gradient	The degree of difference in the power held between the two parties. Results in a balance or imbalance of power. Ch.18
preconditioning	Actions taken prior to discussions to create a link between two events, and designed to influence the other party's thinking or actions. May be positive or negative. Ch.12
predictability	As behaviour is habitual, approach and actions within a negotiation are usually habitual and therefore may be anticipated. Ch.1
price	The price is the amount paid to acquire the product or service or overall deal. Contrast cost. Ch.19
problem-solving	Where both parties have the same problem and the same objective for that problem, a method or process used to find a solution. Ch.2
proposal	An offer made by one party on an issue or variable. The initial proposition should be no less than the optimistic settlement outcome objective. Ch.14
questions	Essential communication tool! Ch.21
range	The limits of a variable's positions – from optimistic to pessimistic (bottom line). Refer variables, position, settlement outcome objectives. Ch.9
ranking	The process of deciding the relative value of each variable based on values and costs to each party. Categorised as aces, swaps or trades, fillers and no-no's. Ch.8
realistic	The most likely settlement outcome objective for a variable. Ch.9
recess	A break in proceedings. Also caucus, adjourn.
relationship	The past and current association influencing the association; the result of

	this negotiation will determine future. Ch.5
remorse	A feeling of regret or concern occurring shortly after the deal is agreed; allayed by a positive reinforcement of decision. Ch.16
ripped-off	A colloquial term for feeling that one has lost in a lose/win outcome. Can be material or emotional loss. Also screwed, done-down. Ch.5
running out	Point where the ability to trade on a variable or several variables is becoming limited. Can be real or perceived – tactic to give impression of running out to reduce the other's demands. Refer trading. Ch.15
sandbagging	A tactic where one party pretends they are weak in order to gain the other party's sympathy and thus achieve strength. Also refer opening gambit.
save face	A behaviour which allows a negotiator to maintain their dignity after making a mistake.
scarcity	A mental approach to the world and the negotiation which views resources as limited. Usually competitive. Compare zero sum. Contrast abundance. Ch.1
screwed	A colloquial expression for feeling that one has lost in a lose/win outcome. Can be material or emotional loss. Also done-down, ripped off. Ch.5
selling	The process within a negotiation where the needs and wants of the other party are satisfied by demonstrating solutions of value; negotiation is the process of agreeing the terms and conditions of providing and accepting those solutions.
shopping list	Each party prepares their own list of issues and variables they wish to include

as part of the transaction. During the discussion stage these lists are developed into a combined list which becomes the basis of the expansion and trading stages. Also refer cherry-picking, straw man. Ch.10

signal — A verbal or non-verbal indication sent consciously or sub-consciously from one party to the other. Ch.20

snowed — A colloquial term for dumping on or being dumped on. Usually refers to feeling overwhelmed or pressured during trading. May refer to a lose/win outcome.

splitting the difference — A tactic used to get a quick decision when trading has reached a point where both parties appear reluctant to move any further. It is a lazy way of trading as it fails to recognise value. May be appropriate if difference is small and helps movement in other areas.

stalemate — Another term for deadlock. Ch.17

stall — A tactic to slow down or delay the negotiation; may occur at any time but usually during bargaining. Ch.17

stonewalling — A tactic where one party refuses to budge from their last stated position. Can be countered by the same tactic, or by breaking off the negotiation.

strategy — The big picture plan of approach to the whole negotiation. Compare tactic. Ch.3

straw man — An item or demand on a shopping list which is not required, but is included to conceal real demands or provide trading ability. Ch.10

style — Negotiating behaviours. Ch.1

swap — Another term for trade. A variable to be traded for items of approximately equivalent value. Refer variables. Ch.8

tactic — Any technique or method used to achieve

	an objective. Often considered as competitive or negative, but in reality the whole process of negotiation involves the legitimate and necessary use of a whole range of tactics.
tactical	The detailed planning and implementation of behaviour at each step of the negotiation process. Ch.3
tag	To put a condition on an offer. Ch.15
tension for change	The effect of the gap between the current situation and the desired outcome. Compare gap, gap analysis. Ch.6
tentative	The language used in a suggested or cautious presentation of a proposal or offer. Ch.14
territory	The place where the negotiation takes place. Best on one's home ground. Ch.13
threat	A competitive tactic intended to influence the other party's behaviour through fear (of consequences of threat being carried out, etc). Compare intimidation. Ch.17
tone	The intangible mood of the negotiation created by the verbal and non verbal interaction between the parties. Ch.20
trade	The stage where bargaining or exchanging of variables occurs. Ch.15. Also the category of variable which due to its high value/high cost ranking is swapped or traded for items of approximately equivalent worth. Ch.8
trade-off	Another term for exchanging. Usually refers to a compromise situation rather than a variable-for-variable trade.
ultimatum	A tactic designed to put pressure on the other party to make a decision. Can be in the form of a deadline, or a 'take it or leave it' offer.
value	The worth of a variable to each party. May be real or perceived value. May have

value system	emotional or material value. Ch.8 The relatively permanent core values of a person or organisation which dictates the way they view and conduct negotiations. Ch.1
variable	A item that is able to be traded by virtue of its ability to be changed and which is desired by the other party. Ch.7
wheat and chaff	Unimportant items (chaff) included in shopping list to assist achieving the important items (wheat). Compare straw man.
wheeler-dealer	A person who is regarded as a market trader who looks after their own interests.
win	An approach to a negotiation and outcome that says: 'I will look after my own interests and I expect you to look after yours.' Ch.5
win-squared	An expression used to indicate an outcome that is beyond the expectations of both parties, due to a creative and synergistic negotiation. Ch.2
win/lose	An outcome where one party wins at the expense of the other. A competitive approach. May be material or emotional wins or losses. Ch.5
win/win	An outcome where both parties consider they have achieved their settlement objectives. A collaborative and creative approach to negotiation based on an abundance mentality. May be material and/or emotional wins. Ch.5
wing it	The behaviour, usually habitual, of entering a negotiation with little or no preparation. Relies on natural wit or personality to get through.
wooden leg	A tactic that introduces a limitation that states that further movement for that variable is impossible. A common opening

zero sum gambit but can be used at any stage. An idea or attitude held that there is a limited amount to be shared, and therefore anything one party achieves will be at the expense of the other. A scarcity mentality. Ch.1